KINGSTON, NEW YORK
The Architectural Guide

William B. Rhoads

Contemporary photographs by
James Bleecker

Foreword by
John Winthrop Aldrich

BLACK · DOME
BLACK DOME PRESS CORP.
www.blackdomepress.com

Published in association with
The Friends of Historic Kingston

Published by:
Black Dome Press Corp.
1011 Route 296
Hensonville, New York 12439
www.blackdomepress.com
Tel: (518) 734-6357   Fax: (518) 734-5802

Library of Congress Cataloging-in-Publication Data

Rhoads, William Bertolet.
  Kingston, New York : the architectural guide / text by William B.
Rhoads ; contemporary photographs by James Bleecker ; foreword by John
Winthrop Aldrich.– 1st ed.
     p. cm.
Includes bibliographical references and index.
  ISBN 1-883789-35-4 (trade paper)
  1. Architecture–New York (State)–Kingston–19th century. 2.
Architecture–New York (State)–Kingston–20th century. 3. Kingston
(N.Y.)–Buildings, structures, etc. I. Bleecker, James. II. Title.

NA735.K55 R56 2002
720'.9747'34–dc21
                                    2002033767

Cover: *Kingston from Golden Hill*, c.1853, artist unknown (Rifenbary Family Collection)

Design by Carol Clement, Artemisia, Inc.

Printed in the USA

Kingston from Golden Hill, c.1853, artist unknown (Rifenbary Family Collection)

*F*amiliarity does not breed contempt. On the contrary
the more familiar it is the more rare and beautiful it is.
Take the quarter in which one lives, it is lovely, it is a
place rare and beautiful and to leave it is awful.

(Gertrude Stein, *Paris France*, 1940)

Kingston in 1875 (F. W. Beers, *County Atlas of Ulster*)

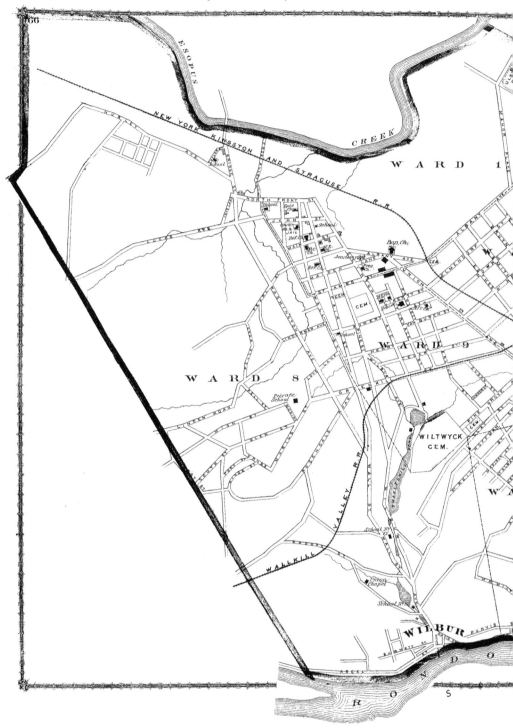

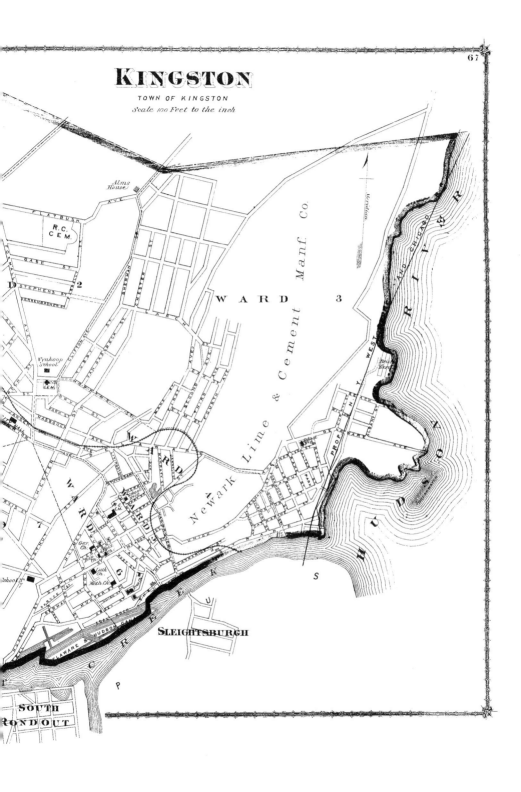

KINGSTON

TOWN OF KINGSTON

Scale 100 Feet to the inch

Kingston in 2002 with boundaries of nine architectural tours.

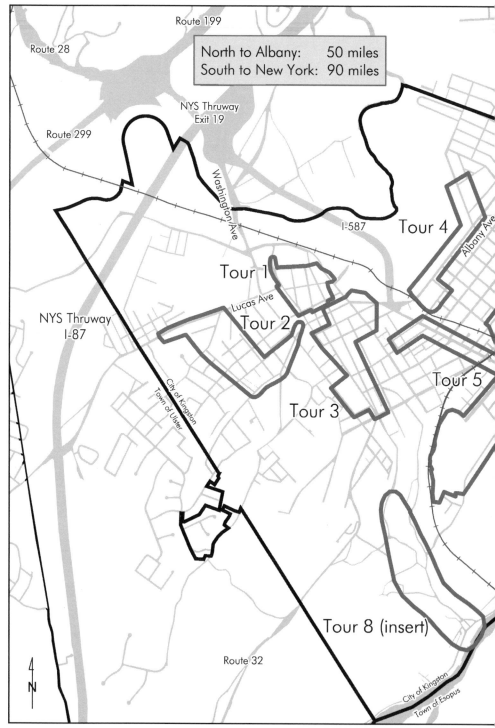

Route 199

Route 28

North to Albany: 50 miles
South to New York: 90 miles

Route 299

NYS Thruway
Exit 19

Washington Ave

I-587

Tour 4

Albany Ave

Tour 1

Lucas Ave

NYS Thruway
I-87

Tour 2

Tour 5

City of Kingston
Town of Ulster

Tour 3

Tour 8 (insert)

Route 32

City of Kingston
Town of Esopus

N

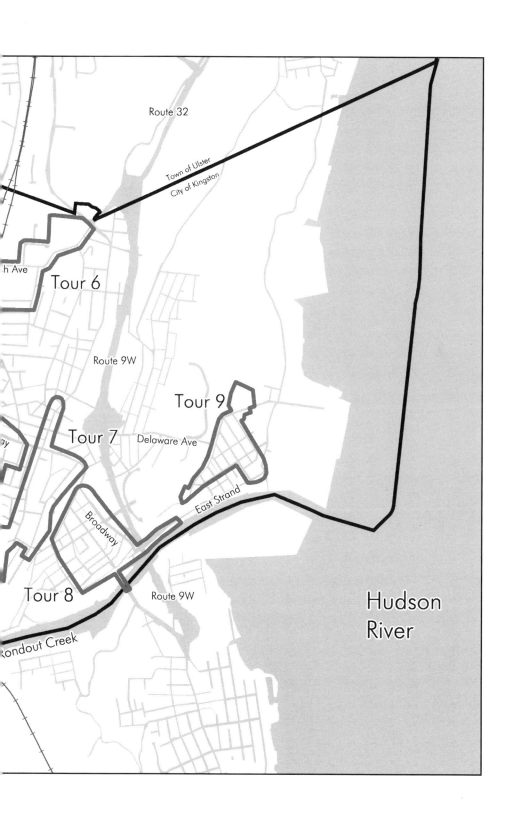

Route 32

Town of Ulster
City of Kingston

h Ave

Tour 6

Route 9W

Tour 9

Tour 7   Delaware Ave

y

East Strand

Broadway

Tour 8   Route 9W

ondout Creek

Hudson
River

CONTENTS

FOREWORD

When I was a youngster in the 1950s, my father, at the helm of his late-nineteenth-century sloop, would occasionally bring my brother and me across to Rondout from our home at Barrytown. After tying up at the bulkhead, we would rummage about in the musty bins and dusty racks of the ship chandlers and purveyors of marine hardware and rope, who had for more than a century given distinctive character to the East Strand waterfront. Soon this was all swept away by the juggernaut of an improved Route 9-W and overreaching schemes for "urban renewal." Years later these memories of what had been needlessly lost spurred me to become a founding board member of the Hudson River Maritime Center in this same historic locale.

It was just this sense of invasive, willful injury done to indigenous architecture and urban heritage fabric that gave rise to the Friends of Historic Kingston (1965) and the achievements of the watershed year, 1966—historic landmarks preservation commissions established by the City of Kingston and the City of New York, and passage of the National Historic Preservation Act, the statute that created the National Register of Historic Places and the State Historic Preservation Office, and delegated to the latter a key role in protecting our built heritage from harm wrought by government itself.

Kingston, New York: The Architectural Guide shows us why such effort deserves to score high in the rankings of civic virtue. There is not one building pictured or discussed in the walking tour portion of this splendid and useful book that the people of Kingston can afford to lose, rich though they be in architectural heritage. Not one! The reader has only to turn to the elegiac pages in the back of the book itemizing what has been lost—the East Strand, the houses designed by Calvert Vaux, the magnificent post office replaced by a Jack in the Box fast-food franchise, among much else—to share the author's deeply felt regret. One closes this succinct book or completes the suggested walking tours feeling a kinship with the prophet Hosea:

> *They have become like those who remove the landmark;*
> *on them will I pour out my wrath like water.*

Fortunately, the climate for historic preservation has improved, in Kingston and throughout the state and nation. The generous program of matching grants provided by New York in recent years, the federal investment tax credit program and other incentives certainly help. Toward this end the nomination of eligible buildings and districts for listing on the National Register continues to be urged But the protection of these resources is not achieved for reasons of the purse alone; the human spirit is lifted by the tangible connection that these buildings and neighborhoods offer—a link back in time to those who pioneered here, building an economy, a community and its institutions, confident in a remote future that is the life we today enjoy, and a link

A *Winter Morning in the Harbor*, photo by Louis E. Jones about 1920 showing Rondout with a ship chandlery on the right.

forward in time to those who will inherit Kingston in an age we will not live to see, a posterity to whom we must feel obliged, in whom we must express confidence by ensuring that the heritage we bequeath to them is a worthy one. The restoration of city hall as the seat of government, the establishment of the Fred J. Johnston Museum and the continuing success of the State's Senate House Museum are all signs that we are on the right course.

This book is another one. It encourages Kingston's residents and visitors to become involved by becoming aware, learning about successive architectural styles, specific Kingston practitioners, patrons, and builders, and by looking at important examples visually accessible to the pedestrian. While commissions in Kingston went to a number of nationally known architects—Upjohn, Vaux, Eyre, and Albro & Lindeberg among them—the central story here is the work of local professionals and of Myron Teller, who was also a recognized pioneer in creating Colonial Revival hardware.

Professor Rhoads and The Friends of Historic Kingston have rendered an important public service in giving us *Kingston, New York: The Architectural Guide*. The diversity of the buildings presented is wide and satisfying. The book's organization, conciseness, and educational value are commendable. The chronology, brief biographies, and other features at the back of the book, and the excellent historic and contemporary photographs, are welcome enhancements. May the reader find inspiration here to become informed, to celebrate, indeed to champion and protect the matchless landmark heritage of Kingston's neighborhoods.

John Winthrop Aldrich
Deputy Commissioner for Historic Preservation
New York State Office of Parks, Recreation and Historic
Preservation

THE FRIENDS OF HISTORIC KINGSTON

Formed in 1965, the Friends of Historic Kingston is dedicated to the following missions: to preserve sites of historic and architectural significance within the City of Kingston, to educate the public about the heritage and beauty of the city, and to acquire and conserve materials relating to local history. The Friends of Historic Kingston received its charter as an educational organization from the New York State Board of Regents in 1970.

A major focus of our organization is the building restoration program, which includes the purchase, renovation, and resale of threatened historic properties within the city. We have successfully renovated four properties: 95 John Street, the Dr. Luke Kiersted House (1972-1973); 20 John Street, the Macauley-DeWitt House (1977-1978); 15 Hone Street, the Thomas Burgess House (1979-1981); and 292 Clinton Avenue, the Amelia Westbrook House (1999).

The Friends of Historic Kingston has taken the lead in conducting inventories and nominations for the New York State and National Registers of Historic Places, resulting in the designation of the districts and individual listings enumerated on page 14. We have published several brochures on these projects.

Frog Alley Park on North Front Street is owned and maintained by the Friends. The park includes the Louw-Bogardus House ruin and the Stockade replica fence with interpretive signage. We also oversee the maintenance of the Sharp Burying Ground on Albany Avenue with an ongoing monument restoration program.

The Friends administers two museums at 63 Main Street. The Fred J. Johnston Museum, a Federal-style house (c. 1812), features eighteenth and early-nineteenth-century furnishings in eight elegant room settings, as well as a period garden; and the adjacent Friends of Historic Kingston Museum houses the headquarters of the organization, a gallery of changing exhibits, local history archives and a gift shop. Activities include house tours, guided walking tours of the 1658 Stockade District and of Rondout, lectures, and special events.

We are proud of our active role in helping preserve city hall and other city landmarks. Now, in our thirty-seventh year, the publication of this guidebook to the city of Kingston represents a highpoint in the history of our organization fulfilling its mission. We are deeply indebted to William Rhoads for his countless hours of research and his keen insights into our architectural legacy.

Jane Kellar
Executive Director

Friends of Historic Kingston rallying to save City Hall, 1975.

NEW YORK STATE AND NATIONAL REGISTERS OF HISTORIC PLACES, KINGSTON, NEW YORK

Clinton Avenue Historic District, 1970

Senate House, 1971

Kingston City Hall, 1971

West Strand Historic District, 1974

Kingston Stockade Historic District, 1975

Broadway Community Theatre, 1979

Rondout West Strand Historic District, 1979

Kingston/Rondout 2 Lighthouse, 1979

Ponckhockie Union Chapel, 1980

Cornell Steamboat Company Shops, 1980

Chestnut Street Historic District, 1985

Kingston City Library, 1995

The Van Steenburgh House, 1999

The Julia Dillon House, 2000

Fair Street Reformed Church, 2001

Boice House, Chichester House, and Kenyon House on Fair Street, 2001

KINGSTON CHRONOLOGY

10,000–9,000 B.C	Paleo-Indian occupations of land near Kingston Point.
1609	Henry Hudson, aboard *De Halve Maan*, arrived at Kingston Point.
1614	Fort-trading post established at Rondout by United New Netherland Company.
1652	Treaty between Esopus Indians and Thomas Chambers for seventy-six acres of land along Esopus Creek.
1658	Petrus Stuyvesant, Director General of New Netherland, orders settlers to move to central fortified location, now uptown Kingston, because of friction with Esopus Indians. Stockade built. Stuyvesant names area Wiltwyck (Wild Retreat).
1659	Start of First Esopus War in September.
1660	July 15. Peace negotiated between Stuyvesant and Esopus Indians.
1663	June 7. Beginning Second Esopus War; twelve of Wiltwyck's houses burned.
1664	England took control of New Netherland, which became New York.
1669	Name of Wiltwyck changed to Kingston.
1777	New York State Constitution drafted and adopted at Constitutional Convention in Kingston. First public reading on April 22 on steps of the Ulster County Court House, Wall Street. New York State Senate convened in home of Abraham Van Gaasbeek.
1777	July 30. General George Clinton elected and sworn in as first governor of New York State in Kingston.
1777	October 16. Kingston burned by British regiment led by Major General John Vaughan, who called the town "a Nursery for almost every Villain in the Country."
1827	Sojourner Truth, later a leading abolitionist, petitioned for son's freedom at Ulster County Court House.
1828	Delaware and Hudson Canal Company established terminus at Rondout. Village became center for shipping grain, coal, bluestone, cement, and brick.

1844	Newark Lime and Cement Company established in Rondout.
1852	John Vanderlyn, the artist, died at Kingston Hotel, Crown Street.
1861	April 18. 20th Regiment paraded in Academy Green, marched to Rondout, and departed for service in Maryland.
1862-1865	120th Regiment, commanded by Colonel (later General) George H. Sharpe, took active part in Battle of Gettysburg and other engagements with the Army of the Potomac.
1870	Ulster and Delaware Railroad (originally Rondout and Oswego) began service, followed by Wallkill Valley Railroad (1872), West Shore Railroad (1883), and New York, Ontario, and Western Railway (1902).
1872	Villages of Kingston and Rondout merge to form City of Kingston.
1887	Senate House State Historic Site established by State of New York.
1893-1897	Kingston Point Park developed by Samuel Coykendall as a major tourist attraction and landing for Hudson River Day Line. Designed by Downing Vaux.
1917	World War I. Hiltebrant shipyard built U-boat chasers.
1941	December 10. World War II. Home Defense Council issued air raid instructions.
1945	March 29. Staff Sergeant Robert H. Dietz of Kingston killed in action in Germany. Posthumously awarded Congressional Medal of Honor.
1955	IBM built Kingston plant.
1961	Urban Renewal Plan instituted with Lower East Project demolition in Rondout.
1965	Friends of Historic Kingston formed.
1966	Historic Landmarks Preservation Commission approved by Common Council, City of Kingston. Fred J. Johnston appointed first chairman.
1970	Post Office, Broadway at Prince Street, demolished.
2000	City Hall restoration completed.

INTRODUCTION

Kingston is a city richly endowed with architectural landmarks set within distinctive neighborhoods. The city has much to offer the curious visitor: venerable stone houses rooted in Kingston's colonial and Revolutionary past on shaded streets in the Stockade District; Victorian-era cast-iron-fronted commercial buildings in Rondout; dignified late-nineteenth and early-twentieth-century houses on West Chestnut Street and Albany and North Manor Avenues; and historic industrial buildings near the Rondout Creek and West Shore Railroad. Even the long-term resident who approaches familiar stretches of the city with alert eyes and inquisitive mind may come away with new insights. These insights may be about the progression of architectural styles over time, but they may also be fresh understandings about the people and changing culture of the city.

For more than a century, Kingston's oldest stone buildings have been valued for their pleasant air of quiet and comforting antiquity in contrast to the frenzied and disturbing modern era. Although it is impossible to connect any existing building with the brief period of Dutch rule of the settlement of Wiltwyck (1652-1664), the stone houses of the eighteenth century also have been treasured for the lessons they teach about the virtues of the courageous men and women who established this nation. The Senate House, the meeting place of New York's first elected Senate in 1777, was acquired by New York State as an historic site and patriotic shrine in 1887. Then, in 1905, the Daughters of the American Revolution acquired the eighteenth-century Sleight-Tappen house as both a meeting place and enduring memorial to their revolutionary forebears. But patriotism and ancestral piety were not always sufficient to preserve old stone houses: in 1873, a landmark on Wall Street built in 1781 was torn down, creating "much interest among the loungers and antiquarians, who watch . . . in expectation of seeing some relic of old times." (*Freeman*, May 7, 1873)

The post-revolutionary economic history of Kingston and Rondout (villages which joined to form the City of Kingston in 1872) also can be traced through surviving buildings. This is especially so of the growth of Rondout following the opening of the Delaware and Hudson Canal in 1828, with further expansion caused by the development of the cement, bluestone, and brick industries in the mid-nineteenth century. Prosperity in the early 1870s resulted in a building boom in both Kingston and Rondout as the two villages were consolidating.

The Newark Lime and Cement Company opened a quarry in 1844 on a steep hill adjoining Rondout village, and by 1851 the company operated a plant nearby to process cement. Long-unused lime kilns can still be seen along Abeel Street near the Rondout Creek, and the ruin of a Newark Lime and Cement concrete barn stands like a roofless sanctuary on the hillside above the Rondout on a part of Union Street where nature is reasserting control. The same company's ambition to assure a constant and moral work force resulted in the Children's Chapel, built of reinforced concrete, which still functions as a place of worship in Ponckhockie.

Iron foundries had an important place in Kingston's economy in the late nineteenth century, as we are reminded of by the surviving cast-iron storefronts with molded panels marked "Rondout Iron Works." These facades told customers that here was a stylish, up-to-date merchant. In 1892, Stock and Rice's New Furniture Store advertised that Kingstonians should "go to 63-70 Union Avenue [now Broadway; the buildings do not survive] . . . where you will see a big iron front building, in which is kept the largest and most complete line of furniture in the state."

The bluestone industry was dependent upon quarries elsewhere in Ulster County, but the cutting and shipping of the stone was done along the Rondout. In 1870, at the peak of Rondout's prosperity, the handsome office of the S. and W. B. Fitch bluestone enterprise, with its distinctive cupola, was built as an advertisement of the stone sent to New York City from the adjacent wharf. Brick manufacturer John H. Cordts's hilltop brick house still surveys the Hudson River, while an office of the Hutton Brick Company remains near the river's edge.

Through his Cornell Steamboat Company and leading role in regional railroads, particularly the Ulster and Delaware, Thomas Cornell was the dominant figure in Rondout's business life in the late nineteenth century. While there are few architectural traces of Cornell's railroads remaining in the city, the steamboat company's boiler and repair shops still stand, and the boiler shop still functions as an industrial building.

The arrival of the West Shore Railroad in 1883, its tracks running through the middle of the city, made that district desirable for industry. See, for example, the Diamond Truck and Car Gear Company on Gage Street (1898) and United States Lace Curtain Mills on Foxhall Avenue (c. 1903) along the rail corridor.

Architecture also provides physical evidence of the coming to Rondout and Kingston of large numbers of immigrants from Europe, who made possible the commercial and industrial growth of the nineteenth-century communities. While long-established Kingston families worshipped in Uptown Kingston at Minard Lafever's Old Dutch Church (1852), whose Georgian forms may have been chosen to refer to the congregation's colonial origins, the Irish in Rondout worshipped at St. Mary's Roman Catholic Church on Broadway, with its Gothic Revival design by Patrick Keely. A few blocks away, St. Peter's Church was built in a German medieval round-arched style for German-speaking Catholics in Rondout. A building of similar German medieval style sheltered the German Lutheran Church of the Holy Trinity. The Polish Catholic community centered around the Church of the Immaculate Conception (1896) on Delaware Avenue. The eclectic, somewhat "exotic" style of Temple Emmanuel helped define Jewish worship as distinct from Christian; its round-arched style relates to earlier German synagogues and to the German roots of Rondout's late-nineteenth-century Jews.

Kingston's cemeteries also demonstrate the range of the population's national origins and religious faiths. Old Dutch Cemetery was the burial ground of the early European Protestant residents. Wiltwyck and Montrepose, picturesquely landscaped cemeteries of the mid-nineteenth century, were again mainly for Protestants, but with sections for Jews. In the nineteenth century, Catholic burials were divided like the churches—St. Mary's Cemetery mainly for the Irish, and St. Peter's for the Germans. African-American burials, after the Civil War, were set apart in the picturesque, hillcrest setting of Mount Zion Cemetery.

* * *

This is the first architectural guidebook to Kingston that aims to draw attention to the broad range of surviving structures designed prior to 1950 within the city limits. I chose the year 1950 as the cutoff point because I find it difficult to assess the historic importance of more recent buildings. The second half of the twentieth century saw the arrival and departure of IBM as the largest employer in the Kingston area, as well as the destruction of the heart of Rondout for urban renewal, and the migration of the major shopping district to a strip outside the city. Architecturally, modernism triumphed over the historical revivals when the Ulster County Office Building on Fair Street was built in 1963-1964 according to an International Style design by Augustus R. Schrowang, Sr., and Augustus R. Schrowang, Jr. Defeated was the Georgian Revival plan of Harry Halverson. Nevertheless, many Kingstonians still preferred the

Ulster County Office Building designed in the International Style by Augustus R. Schrowang, Sr., and Augustus R. Schrowang, Jr., erected 1963-1964.

**Teller and Halverson's proposal (designed by Harry Halverson but not built)
for the Ulster County Office Building using the Georgian style, about 1945.**

Georgian for their homes or institutions, as was the case with the remodeling of the Kingston Savings and Loan Association (1966) on Wall Street by Albert E. Milliken.

Kingston is fortunate to have an abundance of buildings deserving recognition. What criteria were used in selecting the relatively small number for this guide? The focus is on architectural design, not on the history of government or the lives of famous people, unless that history or those lives relate to architectural landmarks. Thus, sites and buildings associated with the origins of New York State, George Clinton, Sojourner Truth, or Father Divine have been only briefly mentioned. Further, I have tried to include many different building types—houses, places of worship, schools, institutions, as well as commercial, industrial, and governmental structures—distributed throughout the city over more than 250 years.

The early stone houses of Kingston deserve a book of their own based on a detailed and probing analysis of their structures by a scholar well-versed in Hudson Valley vernacular architecture. While a number of churches have been included in the guide, a number of interesting examples have had to be omitted. The same can be said of several other categories: cast-iron-fronted stores, Queen Anne and Tudor houses, to name a few.

More than a few buildings of great visual appeal do not appear among the tours because it proved difficult to discover such information as their dates of construction and original owners. Such was the case with the stone house at 169 Albany Avenue, often called the Jacob Ten Broeck house; the bracketed row houses on Henry Street near Broadway; the nineteenth-century workers' housing on Adams Street; and the mansarded and Queen Anne houses on Stuyvesant Street.

Several houses of real architectural interest have been excluded from the tour section because they are difficult to see from the street. An old stone house was destroyed, but elm trees were spared in planning the F. G. Schmidt house (1909) by Albro and Lindeberg, and today the house remains well-screened from North Manor Avenue.

Heavily altered buildings have generally been excluded. The original form of the Kingston Academy at 35 Crown Street is hard to detect, though it is pleasant to enjoy Mexican food within the remodeled remnants of the old stone walls. The Charles Bray house at 262 Broadway was designed by George Evertson Woodward (1829-1905), a prolific publisher of house designs following the example of Andrew Jackson Downing, but the form of the exterior has been muffled by twentieth-century siding. The Opera House, on the corner of Fair and John Streets, by J. A. Wood has lost its mansard roof, its crowning glory. While the Knights of Columbus building on Broadway, designed by Charles Keefe, is largely intact, the replacement of the original front door wholly transforms the impression the building makes on the viewer. Gerard Betz's design for the Ruzzo Bowlatorium at 27 Grand Street, described by Mayor Oscar V. Newkirk at its opening in 1949 as "a showplace and landmark," was thoughtfully transformed into medical offices in 2000; however, without its original function and signage over the entrance, the exterior has lost its character.

Buildings chosen for the guide are, as a rule, easily visible from the sidewalk or street. Readers should keep in mind that a building's inclusion here does not mean that permission has been granted to enter private property. We are grateful to the many private citizens who, as caretakers of Kingston buildings, have maintained and preserved so much of the city.

The building entries begin with a number, allowing the location to be found on the map at the beginning of each tour. The name of the building is usually the name of its original owner or occupant. Current owners or occupants may be indicated in parentheses. The current street address is followed by the date of the building's design and/or construction. If the architect or designer is known, that name follows the date. At the end of the entry, buildings regularly open to the public are identified, as are buildings listed on the New York State and National Registers of Historic Places ("NYS and NR" with the year of listing) or Historic Landmarks Preservation Commission—City of Kingston ("HLPC"). The guide has been organized to suggest possible tours to walk or drive through Kingston's neighborhoods. Walking is recommended to experience these neighborhoods much as they would have been in times past.

Dr. Matthew Jansen's late-eighteenth-century house in 1918 when known as the Old Colony Coffee House.

TOUR 1:
UPTOWN STOCKADE
HISTORIC DISTRICT

Kingston's uptown business district of Wall and Fair Streets lies cheek by jowl with the old stone houses standing on streets laid out for the Dutch settlement of Wiltwyck in the seventeenth century. For at least a century, this juxtaposition of the old and new has struck residents and visitors. Mary Isabella Forsyth (1841-1914), civic leader and descendant of an old Kingston family, observed in 1909: "One cannot walk through the streets of Kingston without feeling the force of its past. The families that have lived there, as many have done, since the founding of [Kingston] . . . belong among the quaint buildings, the antique furniture, the crumbling gravestones, the many memorials of colonial days." Forsyth believed that "great as have been the changes that have transformed the quiet village into a rapidly growing city, with modern villas and lines of electric railroad, there is enough of the old spirit remaining to cause the inhabitants to take pride in calling their town 'The Colonial City.'"

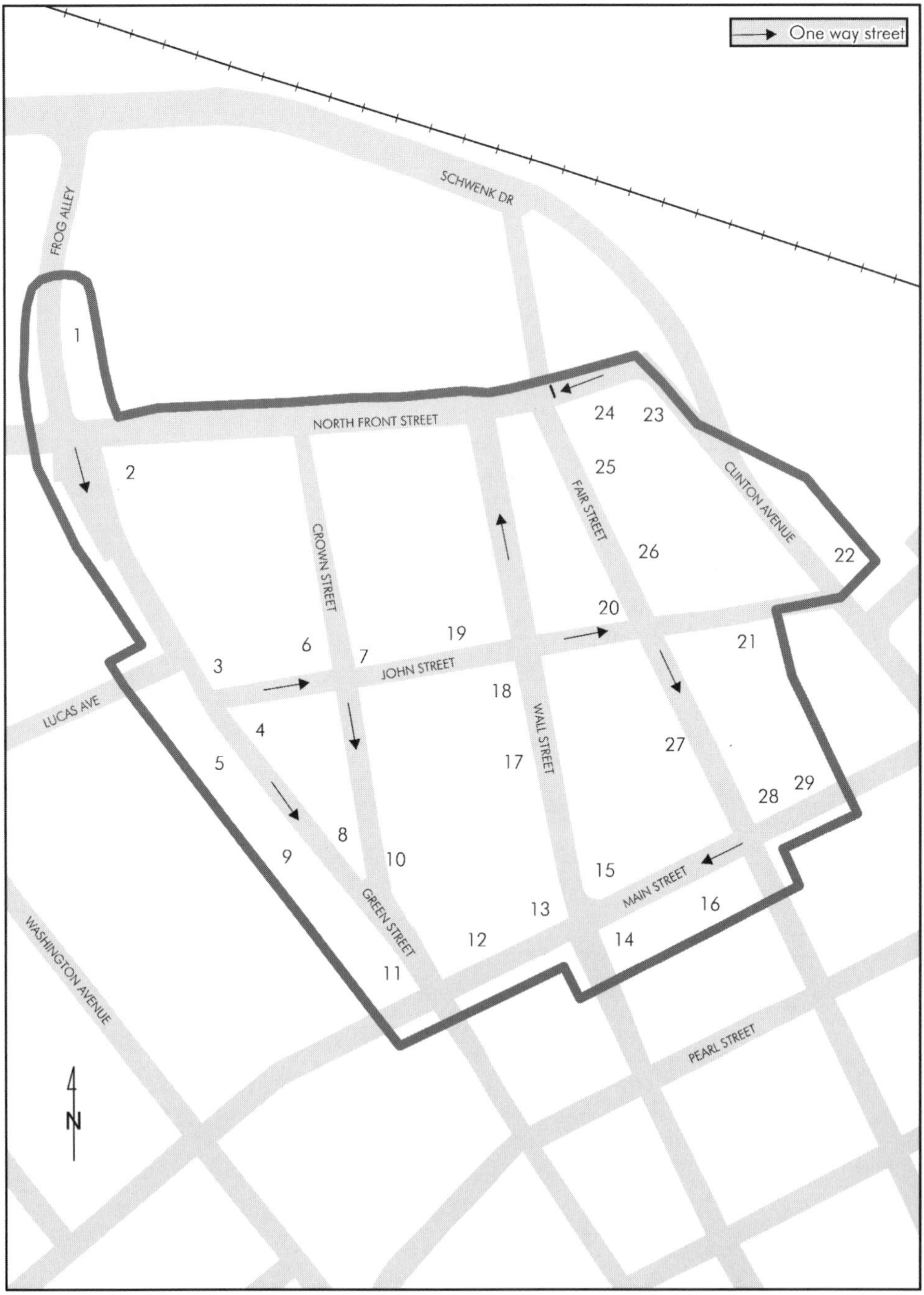
One way street
SCHWENK DR
FROG ALLEY
NORTH FRONT STREET
CROWN STREET
FAIR STREET
CLINTON AVENUE
JOHN STREET
LUCAS AVE
WALL STREET
GREEN STREET
MAIN STREET
WASHINGTON AVENUE
PEARL STREET
N
1
2
3
4
5
6
7
8
9
10
11
12
13
14
15
16
17
18
19
20
21
22
23
24
25
26
27
28
29

TOUR 1:
UPTOWN STOCKADE
HISTORIC DISTRICT

1. **PIETER CORNELISE LOUW HOUSE**
   (Bogardus House; Frog Alley Ruins)
2. **HOFFMAN HOUSE**
3. **DR. LUKE KIERSTED HOUSE**
4. **VAN WEYE-GERRET VAN KEUREN HOUSE**
5. **COLONEL ABRAHAM HASBROUCK HOUSE**
6. **DR. MATTHEW JANSEN HOUSE**
7. **FRANTZ P. ROGGEN HOUSE**
8. **SLEIGHT-TAPPEN HOUSE**
   (Wiltwyck Chapter House of the Daughters of the
   American Revolution)
9. **JUDGE LUCAS ELMENDORF HOUSE**
10. **VANDENBURGH-HASBROUCK-TAPPEN HOUSE**
11. **JACOB TREMPER HOUSE**
12. **DR. JAMES ELMENDORF HOUSE**
13. **JOHN SUDAM HOUSE**
    (Friends of Historic Kingston, Fred J. Johnston Museum)
14. **REFORMED PROTESTANT DUTCH CHURCH**
    (St. Joseph's Roman Catholic Church)
15. **DUTCH REFORMED CHURCH**
    ("Old Dutch Church")
16. **WILTWYCK INN**
17. **ULSTER COUNTY COURTHOUSE**
18. **THE CLERMONT AND THE CORDTS**
19. **THE MOHICAN MARKET**
20. **THE STUYVESANT HOTEL**
    (Rural Ulster Preservation Company)
21. **MACAULEY-DEWITT HOUSE**
22. **J. AMELIA WESTBROOK HOUSE**
23. **THE SENATE HOUSE**
24. **SENATE GARAGE**
    (Ertel Engineering Corp.)
25. **SENATE HOUSE MUSEUM**
    (Senate House State Historic Site)
26. **DR. ROBERT LOUGHRAN HOUSE**
    (Senate House State Historic Site)
27. **WILTWYCK HOSE COMPANY**
    (Volunteer Firemen's Hall and Museum of Kingston)
28. **KINGSTON NATIONAL BANK**
29. **DR. ELBERT H. LOUGHRAN HOUSE AND OFFICE**

1. PIETER CORNELISE LOUW HOUSE
(Bogardus House; Frog Alley Ruins)
North Front Street and Frog Alley
1665-1690 and later

Helen Wilkinson Reynolds, author of the seminal work, *Dutch Houses in the Hudson Valley before 1776* (1929), studied the Louw house before it fell into ruin. According to Reynolds, the eastern portion of the house, probably dating from 1665-1690, was typical of early settlers' houses, built of crude masonry with one room above another, in this case on sloping ground just outside the northwest corner of the Stockade District. The western portion may be eighteenth century. The entire house was burned by the British in 1777. An oblong, stone addition was constructed to the north at an unknown date. (In the 1920s the wood trim was described as recent.)

A fire gutted the house in the 1960s. In 1969 the New York State Historic Trust performed archaeological investigation and testing of the site, and a report by Paul R. Huey describes "a layer of mixed broken red bricks, plaster, mortar, and charcoal," at a level apparently representing "a destruction about the time of the Revolution."

In 1975, the decaying house was threatened with demolition by the Kingston Urban Renewal Agency. Today, the stabilized ruin and adjoining park, a place for the romantic contemplation of the decay of human accomplishments and the survival of nature, are owned and maintained by the Friends of Historic Kingston.
NYS and NR 1975; HLPC

1. Pieter Cornelise Louw House (vintage photo)

2. HOFFMAN HOUSE
94 North Front Street at Green Street
c. 1700 and later

In 1707, the earliest portion of this house, perhaps built in the late seventeenth century, was deeded by Antoine Crespel to his daughter Jannetje Crespel Hoffman, wife of Nicholas Hoffman. Added to several times, it remained in the Hoffman family until the 1920s when began a long period of occupancy by the Salvation Army. Helen Wilkinson Reynolds pointed to the vertical seams in the stonework of the north façade as a sign of additions to the east and west of the original central section. The fine brick wing to the south is nineteenth century. The house was restored by its present owners in 1977 and opened as a tavern restaurant. NYS and NR 1975; HLPC

2. Hoffman House

3. DR. LUKE KIERSTED HOUSE
95 John Street
c. 1795

This is the only wooden clapboarded house from before 1800 to survive in the Stockade District. The façade of this Federal-style house retains its modillioned cornice and beaded clapboards. Its symmetrical, five-bay façade is endowed with the light-

3. Dr. Luke Kiersted House

ness characteristic of the Federal style. The voids of windows and doors here seem balanced with the wall, not dominated by a heavy wall, as is the case with the roughly contemporary Judge Lucas Elmendorf house (111 Green Street).

Threatened by a proposal to widen the street, the Kiersted house was purchased and restored by the Friends of Historic Kingston in 1973 and then sold to private owners. NYS and NR 1975; HLPC

4. VAN WEYE-GERRET VAN KEUREN HOUSE
138 Green Street at John Street
Eighteenth century, 1923

4. Van Weye-Gerret Van Keuren House

5. Colonel Abraham Hasbrouck House (vintage photo)

Where many eighteenth-century stone houses have façades of five bays—a central door flanked on either side by two windows—this house is exceptionally long, having eight bays—seven windows and an off-center door—facing Green Street. The origins of the house extend back earlier than 1711 when Hendrick Van Weye's children sold their father's house. Through much of the eighteenth and nineteenth centuries the house was owned by the Van Keuren family. It burned in 1776 in an accidental blaze, and, after being rebuilt, was soon burned again by the British in 1777.

According to the Historic American Buildings Survey in 1972, the stone portion of the Van Keuren house was built in two stages. The north section consists of six bays, with a door in the fourth bay from the north opening into a stair hall. The smaller south section has two bays—originally the north window was a doorway to the street, as is indicated by the filled-in stonework. A stone partition wall separates the six-bay and two-

bay sections, but it is not known which section is earlier.

Myron S. Teller, who restored the house for Mr. and Mrs. W. Anderson Carl in 1923, found beams slightly charred by the 1777 fire. Teller's drawing for the restoration of the Green Street front indicates new chimneys, dormer windows, porch roof, wrought-iron railing, and sash within the repaired window frames of the old stone house.

NYS and NR 1975; HLPC

5. COLONEL ABRAHAM HASBROUCK HOUSE
135 Green Street
Eighteenth century

Remarkably tall and long for a one-story stone house, this is actually a double house. It was owned by Colonel Abraham Hasbrouck when it was seriously damaged by a fire in 1776, and again when it was burned by the British in 1777. The front

6. Dr. Matthew Jansen House (vintage photo)

doors would always have been entered via Dutch stoops; the bracketed roofs over these doors appear to date from the second half of the nineteenth century, as does the stone gable with paired Gothic-arched windows. NYS and NR 1975; HLPC

6. DR. MATTHEW JANSEN HOUSE
43 Crown Street
Late eighteenth century

The Jansen House was erected after the Revolution on the site of an earlier Jansen homestead. As a two-story, five-bay, hipped roof, stone house, it resembles the Sleight-Tappen house at the junction of Green and Crown Streets, and the Lucas Elmendorf house at 111 Green Street. The fine modillioned cornice may date from the original construction of the house. The low wing to the north served as a doctor's office. In 1918 the building was known as the Old Colony Coffee House, distinguished by the "Sign of

the Golden Coffee Pot" jutting from the stone corner at Crown and Wall Streets. The proprietors, E. D. Williams and M. D. Woodward, embraced the era's enthusiasm for serving simple food, here including "old time griddle cakes," in quaint, colonial surroundings, to people of refinement.
NYS and NR 1975; HLPC

7. FRANTZ P. ROGGEN HOUSE
42 Crown Street
c. 1752

Frantz Roggen, a Swiss immigrant who married Anna Freer in Kingston in 1750, is said to have built this one-and-a-half-story stone house about 1752. Its central doorway and hall may conform to Swiss building tradition. The pair of pointed-arched, Gothic Revival windows in the front gable, the bracketed canopy with pendants over the doorway, and the diamond panes of the door and its flanking windows are nineteenth-century

7. Frantz P. Roggen House

additions that, happily, were not removed by any twentieth-century restoration.

The intersection of Crown and John Streets has a remarkable ensemble of eighteenth-century stone buildings. These include the Roggen house, Matthewis Persen house at 74 John, Kingston Academy at 35 Crown, and Jansen house at 43 Crown.
NYS and NR 1975; HLPC

8. SLEIGHT-TAPPEN HOUSE
(Wiltwyck Chapter House of the Daughters of the American Revolution)
Green and Crown Streets
Eighteenth century

The complex history of this stone house of pre-Revolutionary origin, like so many of its era in Kingston, has yet to be clarified. Traditionally, the building is said to have been begun in the late seventeenth century. Marius Schoonmaker in his *History of Kingston* (1888) identified it as the "homestead of Henry Sleght in the Revolution and at the burning of Kingston." In the nineteenth century it was the residence of John Tappen; he was editor and proprietor of the *Ulster Plebian*, a Democratic newspaper whose office was on the second floor. The low, hipped roof and two-story, five-bay façade appear to belong to the late-eighteenth-century Georgian style. A beehive oven protrudes from the east wall of the kitchen.

In 1905, the local D.A.R. chapter, founded by Mary Isabella Forsyth (1841-1914), voted to purchase the Tappen house as a meeting place. A few members would have preferred the Hoffman house or Wynkoop house. The young architect Myron S. Teller was commissioned to restore the building to its colonial appearance. For architects of Teller's time, restoration meant not an historically accurate restoration, but improvement according to the taste of the current day. In 1907 Teller improved the doorway with a Federal-style transom, side-lights, and porch, including a Dutch divided door and Dutch stoop with settees. Internally, the new work included a staircase based on the one at Woodlawn Plantation in Virginia.

For almost a century, the restored building has stood as an emblem of the sturdy virtues of Kingston's founders, and in accord with the ambition of the D.A.R. to elevate "the minds of the young ... in cultivating a spirit of patriotism and a reverence for the achievements of heroic ancestors," as Judge A. T. Clearwater remarked in a 1906 speech.
NYS and NR 1975; HLPC; open to public

8. Sleight-Tappen House

9. JUDGE LUCAS ELMENDORF HOUSE
111 Green Street
1790s

This large, dignified, two-story, five-bayed, hipped-roof stone house was suitable for a man of Lucas Elmendorf's stature. In 1798 he was elected to Congress, and was re-elected twice; later he was Ulster County's first judge. In contrast to earlier stone houses, its walls were built of more uniformly rectangular stone blocks, and the central doorway and windows were laid out in the usual Georgian symmetrical scheme, although the stone walls dominate the openings more than they would at this time outside the Hudson Valley. The delicate cornice appears to date from the 1790s. The house's most striking detail, the classical door frame with very bold curving brackets or consoles supporting a projecting cornice, is probably a nineteenth-century addition. As architectural historian Paul Malo has pointed out, the stained or painted glass of the transom and sidelights argue for a mid-nineteenth-century date for the door treatment as a whole. NYS and NR 1975; HLPC

10. VANDENBURGH-HASBROUCK-TAPPEN HOUSE
10 Crown Street
Eighteenth century

While some have suggested that this house is from the late seventeenth century and among the oldest houses in the Stockade District, the Historic American Buildings Survey in 1972 proposed that it was built after 1704 for Gysbert Vandenburgh, and rebuilt after the 1777 fire by Abraham Hasbrouck, Jr. Kingston historian Marius Schoonmaker identified the house as "old" in 1888, but cited no owner before Cornelius Tappen, who occupied it in 1820. The stone lean-to at the rear was built later than the front part of the house. Its façade resembles other American two-story, three-bay town houses of the late eighteenth century; however, the clapboarding of the gables follows Kingston practice as seen in one-story stone houses such as the Van Buren house at 28 Green Street. NYS and NR 1975; HLPC

9. Judge Lucas Elmendorf House

10. Vandenburgh-Hasbrouck-Tappen House

11. JACOB TREMPER HOUSE
Green Street at Main Street
c. 1870

While this monumental stone building within the Stockade District is often called the Jacob Tremper house and dated in the eighteenth century, it probably stems from the late nineteenth century. Certainly its mansard roof with pedimented windows, bracketed eaves, and wonderfully sinuous brackets supporting the roof over the twin doorways on Green Street all belong to the post-Civil War period. The Green Street façade also differs from Georgian precedent in having neither window nor door on the central axis.
NYS and NR 1975; HLPC

11. Jacob Tremper House

12. DR. JAMES ELMENDORF HOUSE
77 Main Street
Eighteenth century

Today, and for more than a century, the façade of the Elmendorf house stands out as a lively, picturesque composition with nineteenth-century Gothic Revival pointed-arched windows in twin brick gables and central dormer. The lower panels of the doors have Gothic Revival quatrefoil moldings. Yet the stone walls of the first story speak of its origins: probably late-eighteenth-century with the balanced configuration of central doorway and flanking windows. Early wooden bars still protect the basement windows.
NYS and NR 1975; HLPC

12. Dr. James Elmendorf House

13. JOHN SUDAM HOUSE (Friends of Historic Kingston, Fred J. Johnston Museum)
63 Main Street at Wall Street
c. 1812

By 1812 those claiming up-to-date taste would have dismissed the sturdy simplicities of Kingston's eighteenth-century stone houses. John Sudam (1782-1835), elected a state senator in 1823, was a friend of Washington Irving (1783-1859) and President Martin Van Buren (1782-1862), who were both guests in this house. Sudam opted for a two-story, five-bay, Federal-style house with refined classical details. Especially notable are the cornices (including those of the gables treated as triangular classical pediments), semicircular fanlight over the front door, and surrounds of the front windows. Architectural historian Paul Malo has called the house "a paragon of the Federal style."

In 1938 the house was threatened with demolition, to be replaced with a gas station. Kingston antiques dealer Fred J. Johnston (1911-1993) borrowed money to buy and preserve the landmark as his residence and

13. John Sudam House

showroom. Upon his death, the Friends of Historic Kingston received the house and its fine eighteenth and early-nineteenth-century furnishings as a bequest from Johnston; the house is now open as a museum of decorative arts from two centuries ago, arranged according to refined, mid-twentieth-century taste.

The Friends has established its offices, gallery, and archive (designed by Scott Dutton in 1999) in the stuccoed building facing Wall Street that Johnston erected in 1960 as his antiques shop. Designed by Albert Edward Milliken, the shop's Federal-style pediment, quoins, and fanlight were meant to be in harmony with the adjacent Sudam house. The door surround was salvaged from a house demolished to provide parking for the former Governor Clinton Market on St. James Street.

NYS and NR 1975; HLPC; open to public

14. REFORMED PROTESTANT DUTCH CHURCH (St. Joseph's Roman Catholic Church)
Main Street at Wall Street
1832, 1869, 1898
Henry Rector, J.A. Wood, W.J. Beardsley

This Kingston landmark is a much-altered brick structure that has served remarkably diverse functions: Protestant church, armory, and finally Roman Catholic church. Originally built in 1832-1833 as the Reformed Protestant Dutch Church, the design was by the Albany architect Henry Rector. Best known for designing State Hall (1832-1842; later altered and now the New York State Court of Appeals), Rector was also the architect of the Kingston Academy (1830-1831) that once stood on Academy Green. Thus, at least by 1830, Kingstonians were

33

beginning to turn to architects from outside the community—Albany, and later New York—for the design of major buildings. Rector's Kingston church was essentially Greek Revival, including a two-story, pedimented façade with a frieze of triglyphs (a three-pronged molding) on both front and sides. The panoramic view of Kingston painted in the early 1850s (reproduced on the cover) depicts the church as red brick with white classical trim and white tower. Rector may also have planned the Greek Revival parsonage (built 1837) next to the church at 52 Main Street.

In the 1850s the Dutch Reformed congregation moved across Main Street into its present building, which was designed by Minard Lafever. During the Civil War, the abandoned church served as an armory. The structure again served as a place of Christian worship when, in July 1869, St. Joseph's Roman Catholic Church dedicated its newly-altered building. Changes, designed by J. A. Wood, included an extension at the rear with Romanesque corbel tables and drip moldings. St. Joseph's use of the former Protestant church initially met with a mixed reception. Monsignor Richard L. Burtsell wrote in 1907 that "it is hard for us today to understand the excitement and agitation caused among the people of the staid old Dutch town at the prospect of having a Catholic Church in their very midst, especially so when it was known that a building once used for their own worship was to be occupied for the celebration of mass."

The mansarded, Second Empire-style rectory was added in 1875. A new façade designed by Poughkeepsie architect William J. Beardsley (who earlier had designed the Episcopal Church of the Holy Cross on Pine Grove Avenue) was applied to the church in 1898. It retained the pedimental form of the 1832 building, but added Gothic Revival arches and a low, corner tower. NYS and NR 1975; HLPC

14. Reformed Protestant Dutch Church

15. DUTCH REFORMED CHURCH ("Old Dutch Church")
272 Wall Street at Main Street
1850-1852
Minard Lafever

The heart of the Stockade District is appropriately occupied by the serenely beautiful colonial graveyard and stately, bluestone church edifice of Kingston's oldest religious body, the Dutch Reformed Church, established in 1659-1660. Minard Lafever was commissioned to design a new church across Main Street from the previous Greek Revival building, now altered and serving as St. Joseph's Roman Catholic Church. Lafever, a New York architect and author of much-consulted architectural handbooks, was typical of his eclectic era in designing in a variety of historical styles: Greek, Gothic, or, as here, English Renaissance. Lafever departed from the Gothic Revival often chosen for rival Episcopal and Roman Catholic churches, and recently chosen by Second Reformed for its Fair Street church.

The round-arched windows, and especially the rich classical details of the vaulted interior, derive from the English church tradition of architects Christopher Wren and James Gibbs, as well as eighteenth-century

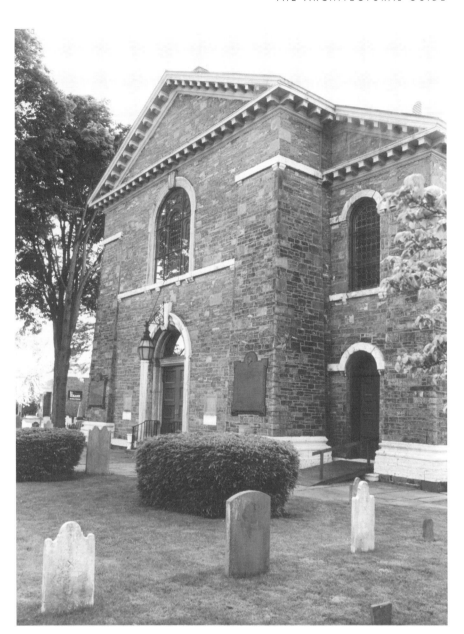

15. Dutch Reformed Church

American Georgian churches like St. Paul's Chapel in New York. The choice of style may have been the request of the consistory or ruling body of the congregation in an effort to separate themselves from their local rivals and to express the antiquity of their American roots, evident in the eighteenth-century tombstones in the churchyard. Fortunately, the London churches of Wren and Gibbs sanctioned a Renaissance design with a tall,

Gothic-proportioned steeple. The original steeple was blown down Christmas Eve 1853 and rebuilt in 1861 (Edward Brink, architect), twenty-two feet shorter, but still tall enough to provide a memorable silhouette for Kingston's skyline even today. Inside the church, a fine Tiffany window rises behind the high, central pulpit.

The classical monument with obelisk in the churchyard near the corner of Main and Wall Streets was originally erected in the Congressional Cemetery in Washington over the grave of George Clinton (1739-1812), Governor of New York and Vice President of the United States. In 1908, the lead casket and the monument with its portrait medallion were moved with great ceremony to this site. Near the corner of Main and Fair Streets stands *Patriotism*, a classically draped woman with a bit of Old Glory clasped to her bosom. The statue, by B. M. Pickett, was presented by General George H. Sharpe (1828-1900) as a memorial to the men of his regiment, the 120th Infantry, New York Volunteers. NYS and NR 1975; HLPC

16. WILTWYCK INN
48 Main Street
c. 1910
Myron S. Teller

Wiltwyck Inn, named after the seventeenth-century Dutch village that later became the city of Kingston, was designed by Teller with brick walls and stepped gables associated with seventeenth-century Dutch architecture in the Old and New World. While New Amsterdam (later New York) and Fort Orange (later Albany) had stepped gabled buildings, Wiltwyck probably never did, certainly not on the scale of the Wiltwyck Inn. Just as Washington Irving added stepped gables to an old Dutch house to create his own home, Sunnyside, in Tarrytown in 1835, so Teller felt

free to invent a stately Dutch inn to face the ancient Dutch graveyard of Old Dutch Church.

The *American Architect* (February 19, 1913), a leading professional journal, praised the inn as "an example of Dutch style of architecture built of a fairly rough textured brick in . . . subdued shades of red, resembling in the general ensemble the old brickwork of Holland." The same journal (August 20, 1913) pictured the inn's brick fireplace and side chairs, both more geometrically Arts and Crafts style in appearance than Dutch.

Teller's client was Miss Mary Kenney, whose inn (also her residence in 1915) was part of a movement early in the twentieth century to provide women with intimate and refined places for tea and luncheons, often with women as proprietors. The Wiltwyck Inn also catered to the automobile touring crowd, as it advertised in the *Automobile Blue Book* (1920) that its dining room and tea room in a "new colonial building" was "noted for home cooking and quick service. Assorted Chocolates and Bons-Bons. Salted Nuts."

While the design of the Wiltwyck Inn may be understood as an expression of Myron Teller's pride in his early Hudson Valley Dutch (Protestant) ancestry, the aura of old Wiltwyck appealed to Kingstonians of varied origins. In 1924 the inn was sold to Aaron and Raphael

16. Wiltwyck Inn

17. Ulster County Courthouse

Cohen, who conducted a real estate and antiques business in the building; an auction of Aaron Cohen's antiques held there in 1927 had refreshments served by the Henrietta Wynkoop Guild of Old Dutch Church. NYS and NR 1975; HLPC

17. ULSTER COUNTY COURTHOUSE
285 Wall Street
1818

Thanks to its generously scaled walls of variously textured stone, its central cupola and pedimented pavilion, and its classically detailed cornice, doorway, and quoins, the Ulster County Courthouse stands as a distinguished example of the late Georgian public building, reflecting the authority and dignity

of the county government. The elliptical arch of the fanlight over the door is characteristic of the Federal style of the 1810s, but there is some question about the date of the cornice whose brackets are bolder than would be expected in the 1810s.

The first county buildings, a courthouse and jail, were erected soon after the incorporation of the county in 1683. A new courthouse was put up about 1732, but was burned by the British in 1777 and subsequently rebuilt. The present courthouse remains on the site of its eighteenth-century predecessor, demolished in 1817. A communication in the *Ulster Plebian* of November 14, 1815, had called for "a more competent building than the present as a court-house and gaol. ... a county of such substantial wealth as Ulster ought in her public business to display a

18. The Clermont (right) and The Cordts (left)

taste which would combine security with beauty and durability."

By the 1890s, the 1818 courthouse was valued as an historic landmark and spared demolition. Andrew F. Mason designed an addition (1897-1898) that did not disturb the front or sides of the courthouse. In 1902, a jail of great blocks of limestone was erected behind the courthouse. On the front lawn are monuments to George Clinton (1739-1812), first governor of New York and vice president of the United States, and to Sojourner Truth

(c. 1797-1883), abolitionist and women's rights advocate.

NYS and NR 1975; HLPC

18. THE CLERMONT
295-299 Wall Street at John Street
1878

THE CORDTS
293 Wall Street
c. 1900

Kingston's grandest surviving commercial building of the nineteenth century, The Clermont, is distinguished for its high mansard roof with iron cresting, great arched window jutting up into the mansard, corbel table below the cornice, and rich color in the brick walls with strategically placed polychrome tiles. The ground-story storefronts, largely of plate glass, are fitted with iron piers having Neo-Grec, shallow fluting. (The Neo-Grec, a mid-nineteenth-century French classical style, was marked by simplified geometric shapes and the shallow fluting seen here.) The bases of these piers are marked "Hermance Bros. Kingston, N.Y."

Next door, at 293 Wall Street, The Cordts shows turn-of-the-century taste for quieter and lighter wall coloration, here primarily yellowish bricks with courses of darker stone. Piers connect the second and third stories, a common compositional pattern in late-nineteenth-century commercial architecture. The metal cornice, brackets, and raised panel with building name are also characteristic of the period.
NYS and NR 1975; HLPC

19. THE MOHICAN MARKET
57-59 John Street
1926-1927
Gerard W. Betz

Planned as "a modern building, specially constructed and fitted out for the grocery, meat, vegetable and bakery business," the Mohican Market's "new modern appliances for the retail business" made it thoroughly up-to-date. The word "modern" as used in Kingston in the 1920s had nothing to do with the stripped and functional "International Style" architecture of the European and American avant-garde. Still, the John Street façade was no longer bracketed Italianate, like so many commercial buildings of the late

nineteenth century, including that next door at 61 John Street. Sturdy brackets were unfashionable in 1926, supplanted by a delicate classical cornice below simple geometric motifs on the roof-line parapet. The geometric motifs are comparable to those of the Central Fire Station on East O'Reilly Street by Teller almost twenty years earlier. Notably "modern" is the vertical sign projecting from the second story and illuminated from within, "a most attractive sign on a background of bright red emblazoned in raised letters of white." (*Freeman*, January 20, 1927)
NYS and NR 1975; HLPC

19. The Mohican Market

20. THE STUYVESANT HOTEL (Rural Ulster Preservation Company)
Corner of John and Fair Streets
1910-1911
J. A. Wood

Among the last works of J. A. Wood, the Stuyvesant lacks the brash coloration and eccentric details of his best work from the 1870s. It appears an attempt to embrace the more sedate, classical taste dominant around 1900 (note the lighter colors of the brick and stone, as well as the conventional details of

Stuyvesant Hotel, Kingston, N. Y.

20. The Stuyvesant Hotel (vintage photo)

the cornice). Still, Wood could not wholly refrain from the old gusto. A domed cupola was designed for the rounded corner entrance, and the capitals by the main door are unorthodox.

An advertisement in the 1920 *Automobile Blue Book* described the Stuyvesant as the "most modern hotel in the Hudson Valley. One hundred and fifty rooms, with hot and cold water and long distance telephone service. Otis elevator. Electric lights. Seventy-five rooms connected with baths. American plan." The Stuyvesant was the hotel of choice when cosmopolitan art connoisseur Charles Freer visited his hometown for several weeks circa 1916.

In 1993 the Rural Ulster Preservation Company renovated the hotel for commercial use and forty permanent residential units, for the elderly, disabled and handicapped. Architects David Smotrich & Partners received an AIA award for the conversion. NYS and NR 1975; HLPC

21. MACAULEY-DEWITT HOUSE
20 John Street
c. 1836

The Greek Revival could take the form of monumental public buildings with columned porticoes, or modest, tasteful houses like the Macauley-DeWitt house. Its Greek aspect is found primarily in the doorway: the square piers and rectangular transom and sidelights. The porch, added later in the nineteenth century, has Italianate bracketed and Gothic cutout details.

In 1931 Alida V. Hibbard, a widow, resided in and operated a restaurant in the former Macauley house. Later it was the home of William C. and Jessie D. DeWitt. He was City Historian and author of the informative *People's History of Kingston* (1943). The house was allowed to decay in the 1970s and was in danger of demolition to make room for a driveway, but in 1977-1978 it was purchased and restored by the Friends of Historic Kingston and then sold to a private owner. NYS and NR 1975; HLPC

21. Macauley-DeWitt House

22. J. AMELIA WESTBROOK HOUSE
292 Clinton Avenue
c. 1831

This small Greek Revival house, with simple classical entablature below the front cornice and classically treated doorway with sidelights, was built by developer Joseph S. Smith, who was associated with the building of the Kingston National Bank at the corner of Fair and Main Streets. The house was long occupied by Amelia Westbrook (1880-1938). It was restored in 1999 by the Friends of

22. J. Amelia Westbrook House

Historic Kingston and resold to a private owner.
NYS and NR 1970; HLPC

23. THE SENATE HOUSE
331 Clinton Avenue
1676 and later

The Senate House has long been treasured both as a birthplace of New York State government and a surviving example of early Dutch architecture. It was here that the State Senate first met in September and October 1777—leading the British to burn the town on October 16.

The building now known as the Senate House is traditionally said to have been built in or shortly after 1676 as the home of Wessel Ten Broeck, and to have been the residence of merchant-trader Abraham Van Gaasbeek when used by the Senate. The building in fact, however, has a more complex history. Ten Broeck's house probably consisted of one room with a gable toward the street. As was common in Ulster County in the eighteenth century, two rooms were added in a linear fashion, with two of the three rooms having doors to the street, placed functionally and not symmetrically. The exterior walls seen today—stone on three sides, but brick laid in English bond on the west—may date from the rebuilding after the 1777 British-set fire. The date of the rebuilding, here, as in the case of other houses burned by the British, remains uncertain.

In 1887 the State acquired the house from Ten Broeck descendants as its second historic site (Washington's Headquarters in Newburgh being the first), and soon added the stone kitchen wing. Isaac G. Perry's design of this wing was meant to harmonize with the old stone house, but such details as the quarter-round windows are not found in local colonial houses.
NYS and NR 1971; HLPC; open to public

23. The Senate House

24. SENATE GARAGE
(Ertel Engineering Corp.)
8-14 North Front Street
1921
Myron S. Teller

The new Senate Garage advertised itself as the "finest garage between New York and Albany." The handsome Dutch Revival façade combines early-twentieth-century commercial design—plate glass and steel-

24. Senate Garage

sash windows and big garage doors—with patterned tile, brick, and stonework, as well as relieving arches above the windows, which were inspired by seventeenth-century Holland. Not surprisingly, the president of Senate Garage, Inc. was named John Van Kleeck and his architect was the devotee of Kingston's Dutch heritage, Myron S. Teller. The tasteful architecture set this apart from ordinary, utilitarian garages, and the desired clientele was elite: sleeping quarters were installed for chauffeurs, and a fireproof safety vault was maintained for tourists' valuables.

Teller may also have designed the patterned brick façade of 254 Clinton Avenue, probably also intended to be Dutch style. In 1922 it was a commercial establishment known as "Doc Smith's Garage"—Dr. Wright J. Smith was a veterinarian.
NYS and NR 1970; HLPC

25. SENATE HOUSE MUSEUM
(Senate House State Historic Site)
Fair Street

1927
Sullivan W. Jones, State Architect; Clarence H. Gardiner, Associate Architect

Governor Alfred E. Smith laid the cornerstone of the Senate House Museum on September 10, 1927. The design was an attempt to create a larger version of a Kingston house at the time of the Revolution, and the fieldstone walls, gable roof, and symmetrical two-story façade do relate to late-eighteenth-century Kingston. Oddly, the profile of the chimney and quarter-round windows facing Fair Street seems to derive from the late-nineteenth-century kitchen wing added by the State to the old Senate House. The interior of the Senate House Museum is notable for its exhibition of paintings and drawings by the important American artist and Kingston native, John Vanderlyn (1775-1852). The elliptical entrance hall was designed to display a portion of Vanderlyn's panorama of the Palace of Versailles, which was later installed in the Metropolitan

25. Senate House Museum (vintage photo)

Museum of Art in New York thanks to the initiative of the philanthropist Emily Crane Chadbourne.
NYS and NR 1971; HLPC; open to public

26. DR. ROBERT LOUGHRAN HOUSE
(Senate House State Historic Site)
296 Fair Street
1873
J. A. Wood

Poughkeepsie architect J. A. Wood designed this Italianate house for Dr. Robert Loughran, a Civil War veteran. The gentle pitch of the roofs, paired brackets, circular window in the gable facing Fair Street, and turned balusters of the porch railing help define the house's Italianate style. The brackets are especially well-detailed with bulbous pendants. It was common practice in the mid-nineteenth century to paint exterior brick walls.
NYS and NR 1970; HLPC; open to public

26. Dr. Robert Loughran House

27. WILTWYCK HOSE COMPANY
(Volunteer Firemen's Hall and Museum of Kingston)
265 Fair Street
1857

27. Wiltwyck Hose Company

The high status of volunteer fire companies in the nineteenth century is evident in the imposing building of Wiltwyck Hose Company. The twin doors opening onto the apparatus floor are twentieth-century replacements, but otherwise the façade is largely intact. The slender bell tower rises as a secular counterpart to church spires in the area. The Italianate arched and bracketed tower overlaps a triangular pediment surmounting the two-story building; the pediment is not Greek, but Italianate, because of the paired brackets that adorn it. The big, second-story window on the right, or north, lit the meeting room and parlor of the company. Within the building, now open to the public as the Volunteer Firemen's Museum, are fascinating displays of fire equipment and original parlor furnishings from about 1880, with medallions incorporating the initials WH. Interior doors have etched glass panels with these initials in complex patterns.

NYS and NR 1975; HLPC; open to public

28. KINGSTON NATIONAL BANK
Main Street at Fair Street
1839

This is the sole survivor of several handsome nineteenth and early-twentieth-century bank buildings in Kingston. American banks of the 1830s were commonly in the Greek Revival style, often with four, six, or even eight columns resembling the façade of a Greek temple. The Kingston National Bank, by using the distyle-in-antis configuration (two rounded columns, in this case Doric, set between squared piers or antae) achieved a

similar effect at lower cost. The Treasury of the Athenians at Delphi (c. 510 B.C.) was distyle in antis, and the bank's classical details in stone may have suggested to Kingstonians that their funds would be securely housed in an institution whose forms, especially the stone columns, recalled the long-surviving landmarks of Greece.

Attached to the bank, to the north, is a structure that originally was a residence facing Fair Street. The center of the five-bay façade once was the doorway. Joseph S. Smith, an officer of the bank and supervisor of its construction, apparently lived in this house.

In 1905 Myron S. Teller designed alterations and additions to the bank, followed in 1927 by Gerard W. Betz's alterations to increase the height of the bank interior by lowering its floor and the entrance on Main Street. The present pair of columns apparently date from this alteration and are taller than the original columns, which were aligned with the surviving antae.

NYS and NR 1975; HLPC

28. Kingston National Bank (photo c.1893)

29. DR. ELBERT H. LOUGHRAN HOUSE AND OFFICE
25 Main Street
1883
Edward Alfred Sargent

Here, the Queen Anne style made its entry into Kingston. By 1883 the Italianate and Second Empire styles were outmoded. The Queen Anne style, derived in theory from picturesque, early-eighteenth-century English houses, favored multiple intersecting roofs, as well as walls composed of various materials. In this case, the upper stories of patterned shingles project slightly over the lower story of brick. Bits of quaint, Queen Anne detailing abound: spindles as a frieze around the recessed porch; a corner beveled off and a delicately pedimented window inserted; other windows placed unexpectedly in corners or with a combination of large and small panes; and panels of leafy scrollwork, one with the date of construction, 1883.

Dr. Elbert H. Loughran was the nephew of Dr. Robert Loughran (see his house by J. A. Wood at 296 Fair Street) with whom he studied medicine. As in the past, Kingston's stylish, up-to-date architecture was provided by a New York architect. Edward A. Sargent (1842-1914) of 58 Cedar Street, New York, signed the drawings for the Loughran house in 1883. About this time, Sargent did architectural watercolor renderings for Calvert Vaux. Three surviving Queen Anne houses on St. Mark's Place, Staten Island, by Sargent in the early 1890s are called "remarkable" by the *AIA Guide to New York City*. NYS and NR 1975; HLPC

29. Dr. Elbert H. Loughran House and Office (vintage photo)

TOUR 2:
UPPER PEARL-MAIN STREET DISTRICT

This district, primarily west of Washington Avenue, encompasses a range of diverse house types from eighteenth-century stone houses to prefabricated houses built soon after World War II. It was just beginning to be intensely developed in 1896 when artist-author R. Lionel DeLisser found "many of the old country roads and lanes still remain . . . shady winding ways much in vogue with the young people of Kingston who are contemplating matrimony." But the rural landscape was fast disappearing, replaced by "many tasty dwellings of modern design." For some years the finely manicured garden of the Burgevin nursery (see adjacent photo) at the head of Pearl Street (now the corner of Pearl and Burgevin Streets) held out against residential development. About 1852, Valentine Burgevin (1819-1899) began the commercial cultivation of flowers, and by 1907 the Burgevin family's nursery had grown to occupy seventeen acres with 50,000 square feet under glass.

Garden entrance to the Burgevin greenhouses at the head of Pearl Street.
(vintage photo)

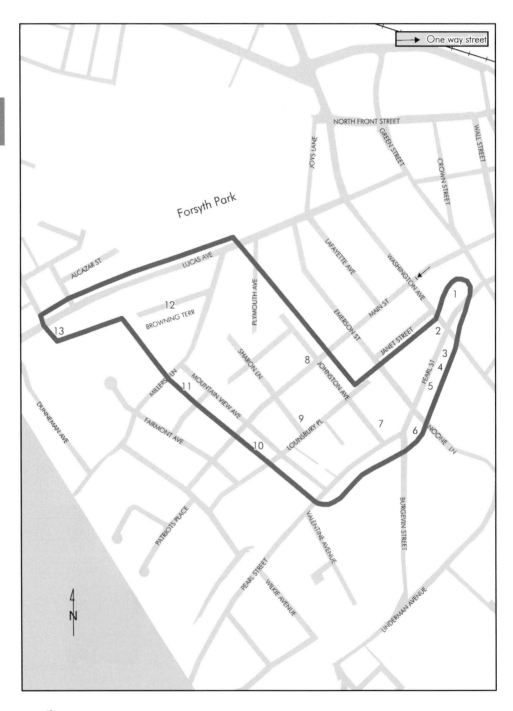

One way street

Forsyth Park

NORTH FRONT STREET

JOYS LANE

GREEN STREET

WALL STREET

CROWN STREET

LAFAYETTE AVE

WASHINGTON AVE

ALCAZAR ST

LUCAS AVE

PLYMOUTH AVE

EMERSON ST

MAIN ST

12

BROWNING TERR

SHARON LN

8

JANET STREET

1

2

3
4

PEARL ST

5

13

JOHNSTON AVE

MILLERS LN

MOUNTAIN VIEW AVE

11

DUNNEMAN AVE

FAIRMONT AVE

9

LOUNSBURY PL

7

6

NOONE LN

10

PATRIOTS PLACE

BURGEVIN STREET

VALENTINE AVENUE

PEARL STREET

WILKIE AVENUE

LINDERMAN AVENUE

N

TOUR 2:
UPPER PEARL-MAIN STREET DISTRICT

2

1. CORNELIUS MASTEN-JULIA DILLON HOUSE
2. HENRY L. ABBEY HOUSE
3. JOHANNES MASTEN-ANNIE E. P. SEARING HOUSE
4. GERARD W. BETZ HOUSE
5. LUKE NOONE HOUSE
6. JUDGE JAMES BETTS HOUSE
7. DELANCEY N. MATHEWS HOUSE
8. ALEXANDER B. AND LOUISE W. SHUFELDT HOUSE
9. STANLEY MATTHEWS HOUSE
10. CONRAD AND HELEN ROBINSON HOUSE
11. JOSEPH LEVINE HOUSE
12. BROWNING TERRACE
13. CHARLES AND GRACE KEEFE HOUSE

1. CORNELIUS MASTEN-JULIA DILLON HOUSE
109 Pearl Street
Eighteenth century with later additions

This house, currently the manse of Old Dutch Church, is perhaps best remembered as the residence and studio of Julia McEntee Dillon (1834-1919), a painter of flowers, and a prominent figure in Kingston society. The building's core is an eighteenth-century stone house. By 1895 Julia Dillon began her occupancy, and probably about that time added a harmoniously proportioned studio room and porch facing Pearl Street. (This appears at the left in the accompanying photo taken in the 1890s.) Vine-covered walls, "ancient trees," and "a garden of old-fashioned flowers" (*House Beautiful*, Nov. 1905) helped create an aura of rural charm that was enhanced by a picturesquely hooded wellhead. Dillon's garden interests led her to publish a booklet, *Old Gardens of Kingston*, in 1915. As a member of the Daughters of the American Revolution, Dillon was drawn to old gardens, houses, and furnishings; her sitting room had a Federal-style mantelpiece, and, among the house's eclectic furniture, were some family heirlooms.

In 1919, soon after Dillon's death, her sisters, Mrs. T. V. R. Brown and Mrs. J. P. Paulding, employed Myron Teller to make alterations and additions. These included a frame wing replacing Dillon's studio and a service wing to the rear of the property. The additions—with their gable roofs, shed-roofed dormers, and simple details—were said to be "conforming with the spirit of the old [colonial] work."
NYS AND NR 2001; HLPC

2. HENRY L. ABBEY HOUSE
133 Pearl Street
c. 1870
This is the best surviving example in Kingston of the Gothic Revival cottage popularized by Newburgh's Andrew Jackson Downing (1815-1852) and Calvert Vaux

1. Cornelius Masten-Julia Dillon House (vintage photo)

(1824-1895). The board-and-batten construction and steeply pitched, intersecting gable roofs are characteristic of the American Gothic cottage, as are the sequence of elements making up the Washington Avenue façade: trefoil cutout at the peak of the gable, second-story oriel window, and hood over the first-story window. The Gothic Revival encouraged odd, even quirky details, like the small circular window sheltered by a five-sided gable. The corner porch was probably a later addition.

Henry L. Abbey (1842-1911), a poet, editor, and flour, feed, and grain merchant, owned the cottage in 1870. Abbey married Mary Louise DuBois, of Kingston, in December 1865, and may have had the home built between then and 1870. Earlier, in the 1850s, the Rondout landscape painter, Jervis McEntee, had occupied a studio in similar style, designed by his brother-in-law, Calvert Vaux (see p. 165). Was there something about small, picturesque wooden buildings that appealed to artists and poets? A similar, but probably later cottage at 7 Lebert Street, located in Jacob's Valley, near Wilbur,

has hooded windows and corner porch in Queen Anne style.

2. Henry L. Abbey House

3. JOHANNES MASTEN-ANNIE E. P. SEARING HOUSE
142 Pearl Street
Mid-eighteenth century and later

3. Johannes Masten-Annie E. P. Searing House (vintage photo)

When Myron Teller was called upon to restore the Masten House, it was, according to Helen Wilkinson Reynolds, "barely weatherproof." Teller's client, Annie E. P. Searing, was an author, poet, and early advocate of woman suffrage. She wrote at length in *House Beautiful* (May 1921) about the 1919 restoration of the neglected "old Dutch stone house she had loved since her childhood," but unfortunately she did not mention Teller's role as architect. Externally, few changes were made: wide, shed-roofed dormers were added to make the second story usable for bedrooms, and a kitchen porch was built with bluestone floor. There she could "shell the peas, string the beans, pit the cherries or just rock."
HLPC

4. GERARD W. BETZ HOUSE
152 Pearl Street
c. 1928
Gerard W. Betz

Architect Gerard W. Betz designed this stone-veneer Colonial Revival house as his own residence. Like Charles Keefe, Betz was no purist in reviving colonial forms. Here he called for flat stones to be laid so that they were clearly not load-bearing, but a veneer, a practice avoided by Teller and Halverson. Regional Dutch tradition probably lies behind the gables with wood above stone, the shed-roofed dormer, and the casement windows (although few of these survived in Kingston's old houses). Betz may have been bridging the Colonial and Tudor Revivals, the latter inspiring the multiple gables (including that over the front door), casement windows, arched door, and generally picturesque composition.

4. Gerard W. Betz House

5. LUKE NOONE HOUSE
172 Pearl Street
1874

The *Daily Freeman* reported on June 2, 1874, that Luke Noone had recently laid the foundation for his handsome house on Pearl Street in his "quarry lot" and that it was to be built of brick and stone. Luke Noone (1822-1905) had learned the stonecutting trade in Ireland from his father, a stone contractor, before departing for America in 1848. Soon he and others established a stonecutting and contracting business in Kingston that provided stone for, among other structures, the Fair Street Reformed Church. Noone's quarry at Mapleton (off Hurley Avenue near Quarry Street) also was a source for the stonework of the Brooklyn Bridge.

The Noone house is a marriage of the concave mansard roofs of the Second Empire style with the picturesque Italian villa, the latter evident in the house's tight-knit asymmetrical massing, and particularly in the three-story tower above the main entrance. (Architectural historian Jane Davies discovered that a house begun for the artist James Smillie in Rondout in 1836, but never completed, was "probably the earliest Italian villa begun in America.") The view from the "observatory" atop the house was said to

5. Luke Noone House

in beautiful mountain scenery in the state." (*Daily Freeman*, October 12, 1874) From the Italian Renaissance are the rusticated (rough-textured) quoins or stone blocks, which accent the corners of the house and would have reminded Noone's contemporaries of the source of his prosperity. The *Daily Freeman* counted four bay windows—part of the "rage" for such windows in the 1870s.

cover "a large portion of Ulster County with that background, the Catskills, unsurpassed

6. JUDGE JAMES BETTS HOUSE
204 Pearl Street
c. 1903

Given prominence by its raised site, the Betts house also stands out as striving to project an aura of dignity through its use of Colonial or Georgian Revival forms. The sym-

6. Judge James Betts House

metrical, five-bay façade of red brick, with white quoins and gambrel roof, resembles eighteenth-century Georgian houses, but the asymmetrical porch and bay window, as well as the idiosyncratic roof dormers and Palladian window of the second story, betray the circa 1900 date of the design.

The property was purchased in 1901 by James Betts from Luke Noone, owner of the nearby quarry and Italian villa whose style was wholly outmoded by 1904. Betts was a prominent Democrat and State Supreme Court judge. Governor Alfred E. Smith spent a "social hour" at the Betts house on September 18, 1920, after laying the cornerstone of the Rondout Creek Bridge.

7. DELANCEY N. MATHEWS HOUSE
207 Pearl Street
c. 1912
Myron S. Teller

Myron Teller's dedication to Dutch or Dutch Colonial architecture is not so obvious in this house, built for the president of the State of New York National Bank, as in his Wiltwyck Inn on Main Street or stone house restorations. Still, the parapet gable facing Pearl Street, the polychrome brick and stone, and the segmental-arched windows were surely intended to refer to the Dutch origins of Kingston. The asymmetrical Pearl Street façade with shadowed roof overhangs resembles the nineteenth-century picturesque, while the broad, simply ornamented walls, and the brick terrace wall joining house and garden relate to the progressive Arts and Crafts spirit of the 1910s. The carriage house/garage is in harmony with the main house in its jerkin-head roof, and mixture of Arts and Crafts simplicity with a few quaint historical details.

7. Delancey N. Mathews House

8. ALEXANDER B. AND LOUISE W. SHUFELDT HOUSE
71 Johnston Avenue
1921
Charles S. Keefe

The gambrel-roofed house with dormer extending across much of the lower slope of the gambrel was a very common design in the early twentieth century, and was popularly known as "Dutch Colonial." The similarity to Dutch colonial houses in the Hudson Valley was, however, slight. Keefe's design for the Shufeldts (Alexander was general manager of Universal Road Machinery Co., manufacturers of heavy equipment) is a compressed, asymmetrical example of the Dutch Colonial house. The Alexander A. Stern house, built by contractor Jay W. Rifenbary at 28 Presidents Place in Rondout in the 1920s, is a more typically proportioned, symmetrical Dutch Colonial. The Shufeldt house's gambrel roof with broad dormer is Dutch Colonial, as was the stoop with benches (not extant) by the doorway. Keefe was not a strict reviver of historical precedent,

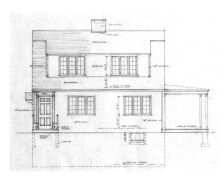

8. Alexander B. and Louise W. Shufeldt House (Keefe drawing)

so he freely mixed delicate Federal pilasters by the door with Arts and Crafts stucco walls and three-part casement windows. Nearby, at 55 Johnston Avenue, is the George A. Winter house (1911), a one-story bungalow by Keefe with no pretensions to historical revivalism.

9. STANLEY MATTHEWS HOUSE
61 Lounsbury Place
1926
Charles S. Keefe

9. Stanley Matthews House

Charles Keefe's modest national reputation was based on his skill in designing simple, practical, and charming Colonial Revival houses. For Stanley Matthews, Vice President of the Kingston Grain Co., Keefe turned instead to the English Tudor style in the stucco walls, casement windows, asymmetry, and cross gable. Still, the essential restraint of the design—there is little ornament and no half-timbering of the kind so often found in Tudor houses—is comparable to Keefe's Colonial Revival work. The metal frames of the casement windows help identify the house as early-twentieth-century.

10. CONRAD AND HELEN ROBINSON HOUSE
55 Mountain View Avenue
1936
Walter Robinson

Lovers of the Tudor and Colonial Revivals in the 1930s must have been shocked by the starkly modern shapes of the Robinson house, designed by eighteen-year-old Walter Robinson for his uncle and aunt, Conrad and Helen Robinson. (Conrad Robinson headed Ulster Fuel Oil Heat and Power Corp.) Walter Robinson had recently arrived from Austria, and in 1991 reminisced that in the 1930s he had been "influenced by the Bauhaus school but could surely not lay any claims of having abided by its philosophy, nor having accomplished its objectives." The flat roof and absolute geometric clarity of the walls and openings punched into them resemble the International Style of the Bauhaus in Germany, but the heaviness of the tawny brick walls goes against the thin glass membrane walls commonly associated with the International Style. The Robinson house seems more akin to the Austrian architecture of Adolf Loos in the 1910s and 1920s.

Walter Robinson served as both designer and general contractor. He recalled that steel was used for lintels and main girders— steel had rarely been used in Kingston resi-

10. Conrad and Helen Robinson House

11. Joseph Levine House

dential construction—and that the steel was purchased inexpensively from a scrap yard on the Strand. After designing this house, Walter Robinson studied engineering at Rensselaer Polytechnic Institute and practiced in Ohio. The roof over the open deck and simple classical posts supporting this roof were not part of the original design, and the garage has been altered.

11. JOSEPH LEVINE HOUSE
105 Mountain View Avenue
1939-1940
Albert Edward Milliken

One of the city's most sophisticated, large residences, the Levine house was built at the end of the Great Depression. It was commissioned by an owner of a newspaper distribution business and the Empire Liquor Store at 600 Broadway, which was graced with a handsome Art Deco neon sign.

The English Tudor style of the Levine house is more fully developed than it was in Keefe's Matthews house. Here, the brick wall is interrupted by groups of steel casement windows with drip moldings above. Multiple roof gables, gabled dormers, and an entrance vestibule combine for a continuation of nineteenth-century picturesque effects. From the outset, vines were to cover the walls and hemlocks were to screen the house from the nearby street, creating something of the aura of an old house in the lovely, English countryside.

12. BROWNING TERRACE
1950-1952
Gunnison Homes, Inc.

The prefabricated houses lining Browning Terrace helped meet the need of World War II veterans, and others, for affordable housing in Kingston. Walter Donnaruma, a 1928 graduate of Kingston High School, and a veteran, obtained a franchise to sell houses made by Gunnison Homes, Inc., a subsidiary of United States Steel, in its New Albany, Indiana, factory. In February 1950, Donnaruma, representing Gunnison Homes, applied to deed to the city a dead-end street to be named Browning Terrace, after local radio newscaster Robert F.

Browning. Twenty-three lots had been sold, each with a house to be produced by Gunnison, sponsor of the project.

Today about twenty Gunnison houses can be identified on Browning Terrace. All have been altered. The one-story, gable-roofed houses at first seem like countless other post-war houses across the country. Several houses, however, retain indications of their Gunnison origins: steel-sash windows and an oval, louvered opening in the gable ends. Oddly, despite the affiliation with U.S. Steel, the houses are essentially wooden, originally with exterior wall panels of waterproof, laminated plywood sheets.

The houses were shipped from New Albany as panels, the walls complete with windows and electrical wiring, and arrived in boxcars via the New York Central and Ontario and Western Railroads. The factory-assembled panels forming walls, ceilings, roofs, and gables could be erected in a day on concrete slabs (there were no basements), while shingling the roof and finishing the inte-

rior might take three days. A two-bedroom house and lot sold for $6,600. Veterans quickly took advantage of 100% mortgages guaranteed by the Federal Housing Administration or Veterans Administration.

Pre-fabrication was commonly believed to be the solution to America's post-war building needs, and not only for housing. The Seventh-day Adventist Church (1946-1947) at 30 Pearl Street was partially pre-fabricated by the Benart Company of Albany Avenue extension. It was said to be the first pre-fabricated church in Kingston. While its construction was novel, it still looked like a traditional Gothic church.

13. CHARLES AND GRACE KEEFE HOUSE
258 Lucas Avenue
1911
Charles S. Keefe

Charles S. Keefe, a native of Kingston and an architect who practiced in Kingston

12. Browning Terrace

and New York, designed this simple Colonial Revival house for himself and his wife Grace. The white clapboarded walls, symmetrical façade, and modest details represented good taste to countless homeowners in the early twentieth century. Aside from the Mediterranean appearance of the chunky columns and trellis at the front door, Keefe's house reflected the period's widespread preference for American colonial design as America's own, national style. Keefe himself wrote in 1926 that the wooden Colonial Revival house "is typically American . . . developed by the conditions and needs of our climate and our ways of living." During the Great Depression, Keefe was obliged to close his New York office and retreat to Lucas Avenue, transforming his bedroom into an office. Following his death, the *Architectural Record* cited him as "a widely known house architect and an authority on Colonial American homes."

2

A Merry Christmas
from
Charles & Grace Keefe

13. Charles and Grace Keefe House (Keefe drawing)

MR. FORSYTH'S HOUSE, KINGSTON, N.Y.

Richard Upjohn's design for the James C. Forsyth house.
(Collection of the Avery Architectural and Fine Arts Library, Columbia University)

TOUR 3:
FAIR STREET HISTORIC DISTRICT

3

The vitality of the city, as it has grown to accommodate a changing culture, is exemplified in the Fair Street District. Here, the dignity of a wealthy family's mid-nineteenth-century mansion, the Forsyths' on Albany Avenue, and of a stately Gothic Revival church, Fair Street Reformed, stand in contrast to landmarks of the first half of the twentieth century: a once common, but now rare, neighborhood grocery, and a sleekly modern gas station now transformed into a bakery on Greenkill Avenue.

Three fine examples of the mid-nineteenth-century Italianate house are clustered at 82, 98, and 104 Fair Street. The three houses are little changed from their appearance in a painted panorama of Kingston (reproduced on the cover) executed in the early 1850s by an as-yet unidentified artist. The Masten family occupied 82 Fair Street in the later 1860s, and Philip V. D. Lockwood, a stone merchant in Wilbur, resided at 98 Fair Street in 1858. Number 104 Fair Street, owned by William S. Kenyon in 1870, was recently added to the New York State and National Register of Historic Places, along with the Fair Street Reformed Church and two mansarded houses, the Chichester House (116 Fair Street) and Hewitt Boice House (110 Fair Street).

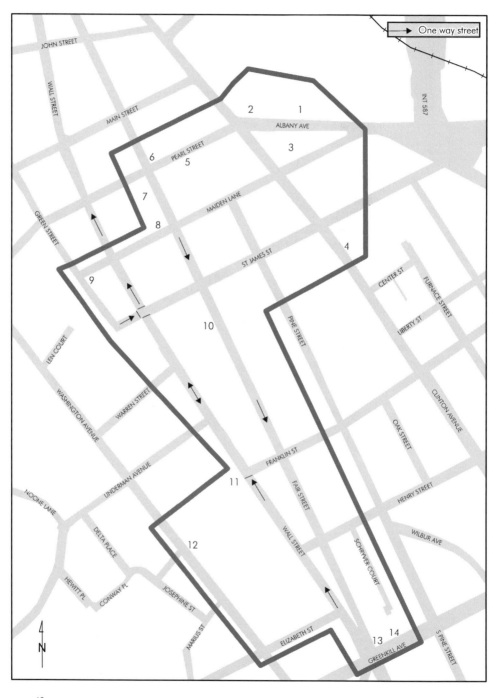

TOUR 3:
FAIR STREET HISTORIC DISTRICT

1. **JAMES C. FORSYTH HOUSE**
      (Masonic Temple)
2. **GOVERNOR CLINTON HOTEL**
      (Governor Clinton Apartments)
3. **ACADEMY GREEN PARK**
4. **EDWARD BRINK HOUSE**
5. **JAMES B. WEEKS HOUSE**
      ("The Columns")
6. **ST. JAMES METHODIST EPISCOPAL CHURCH**
7. **SECOND REFORMED DUTCH CHURCH**
      (Fair Street Reformed Church)
8. **MYRON TELLER HOUSE**
9. **VAN BUREN-GORDON HOUSE**
10. **FIRST CHURCH OF CHRIST SCIENTIST**
11. **TOBIAS VAN STEENBURGH HOUSE**
12. **HOME FOR THE AGED OF ULSTER COUNTY**
      (Hudson Valley Senior Residence)
13. **BOULEVARD GULF SERVICE STATION**
      (Cake Box Bakery and Café)
14. **M. A. WEISHAUPT GROCERY**
      (Charles Grocery and Deli)

3

1. JAMES C. FORSYTH HOUSE
(Masonic Temple)
31 Albany Avenue
1849-1850
Richard Upjohn

1. James C. Forsyth House

This monumental Italianate house was designed by the important New York architect, Richard Upjohn, best known for designing Trinity Church (1839), a Gothic Revival landmark in New York on Broadway at Wall Street. Upjohn considered the Gothic most appropriate for sacred, Christian architecture, so for this residence he used the secular, Italianate mode. The symmetrical façade, low hipped roof, front gable with circular window, and bracketed eaves are Italianate, as are the pedimented and arched moldings above the windows. The unusual boldly-curving braces and the large pendants of the door hoods on the east side originally matched the details of the broad front porch, which projected from the façade unsupported by posts to the ground. (Watercolor drawings by Upjohn's office, preserved in the Avery Library at Columbia University, show the original appearance of the exterior and the floor plan.) In 1939 the house was remodeled for Masonic functions by George E. Lowe, and the present front and east porches with Ionic columns may date from 1939. The nineteenth-century stone gateposts and the cast-iron fence with its arched grill relate harmoniously to the house.

James Christie Forsyth (1819-1855), a native of Newburgh, came to Ulster County about 1840 and was a lawyer, politician and judge. In September 1847 Forsyth wrote his wife, Mary Bruyn Forsyth, (letter in the Archives of the Huguenot Historical Society, New Paltz) from New Haven, Connecticut, where he had seen "a great number of exquisite private residences, distinguished for their finished beauty, convenience, and above all, cheapness." He found houses built for $3000 or $3500 "which are in every respect superior to any in Kingston." He was also impressed with "an architect or rather (to do him only justice) an artist" who had designed a house "like Mrs. Sickles new one," but "more tasty than hers and ... much more convenient." (Mrs. Sickles may have been Ann Sickles, who in 1857 lived on Maiden Lane near Wall Street.) Forsyth wanted to talk with his wife, then have the unnamed New Haven architect "draft a plan and specifications ... Give me these Yankees after all against the world." By 1849, however, the Forsyths turned to the New York architect Richard Upjohn, and husband and wife both corresponded with Upjohn about the construction and furnishing of their house. In May 1851 the Forsyths gave a party at their new mansion, well designed for such events with its 24-by-18-foot dining room and 26-by-24-foot drawing room, set apart from the more intimate parlor and library. Nathaniel Booth, a merchant in Wilbur and a diarist, attended the party:

> ...the Judge's new house is a splendid affair throwing all others in Kingston in the shade.—the delicately carved marbles—the rich carpets—mirrors—paintings and furniture would rather astonish the honest Dutch who built Old 'Sopus could they revisit old scenes—I wonder if they sleep guiltily in their

3

graves while such changes are going on. The amusements of the evening were made up of music, champagne, and oysters, which immortal trio enabled the evening to pass agreeably.

As Stuart Blumin suggests, the "'honest Dutch' . . . soon obtained satisfaction. Two years after his housewarming party, Judge Forsyth fled to England a step ahead of the discovery that his forgeries and illegal stock sales exceeded $200,000." The Rondout *Courier* in 1853 called him "a spoiled child of fortune." His vices included gambling and trying to keep up with Newport and New York society. Upjohn, in fact, had designed an Italian villa (1845-1847) in Newport for Edward King, which may have inspired the Forsyths. James Forsyth died in England in 1855. The Judge's daughter, Mary Isabella Forsyth, spent her childhood in the Albany Avenue house and later acquired a sterling reputation as a civic benefactor through charitable work on behalf of the Industrial Home for Orphan Children, Old Dutch Church, and D.A.R.

2. GOVERNOR CLINTON HOTEL
(Governor Clinton Apartments)
1 Albany Avenue
1924-1926
George E. Lowe

The Georgian Revival façade of the Governor Clinton Hotel recalled the era of George Clinton, but also signaled good taste and domesticity to tourists and business travelers in the 1920s. The three-story, white classical portico far surpassed the low columns of the rival Stuyvesant Hotel located on Fair Street; guests might hope for a level of comfort approaching that enjoyed by owners of antebellum plantations with similar porticoes. Financial considerations doubtless dictated the inclusion of not-very-homey shop windows flanking the portico, but the shuttered upper-story windows reasserted comforting domesticity.

The hotel was built on the site of the mansarded house of Civil War hero General George H. Sharpe (1828-1900). His house was moved to the back of the property in 1924 to serve as a hotel annex. A porch at

2. Governor Clinton Hotel (vintage photo)

the rear of the hotel yielded a broad view of the Catskills; the grounds adjoining the porch were terraced and led to a formal garden. Kingston artist Emily Hoysradt (see p. 126) painted two murals—pictorial maps including such landmarks as the Senate House and Kingston Academy—in the hotel's early-American-style coffee shop.

3. ACADEMY GREEN PARK
Albany Avenue, Clinton Avenue, and Maiden Lane
1918 and later

Academy Green was the site of Kingston Academy from 1830 until 1916, when it was replaced by the new high school on Broadway and was demolished. In 1918 the land was deeded to the city, and it is the principal public space in the center of uptown Kingston. The park provides shaded walks and lawn embellished with sculpture and a fountain.

Several notable houses are found on the perimeter of Academy Green. Across Clinton Avenue, at One Pearl Street, an Italianate house with central cupola was erected in the early 1870s for John S. Burhans. In 1896, it was owned by Judge Alton B. Parker, who became Chief Justice of the State Court of Appeals in 1898 and was the Democratic candidate for president in 1904, but was defeated by Theodore Roosevelt.

On November 2, 1936, Academy Green served as a gathering place for some 7,000 citizens to welcome Franklin D. Roosevelt near the end of his re-election campaign. FDR spoke briefly from his car, genially greeting "my friends and neighbors," and referring to his ancestral connections with

3. Academy Green Park

Ulster County. There was a similar gathering for him here on November 4, 1940. He told the crowd that he had "very close ties with Kingston, because about 270 years ago one of the very earliest Roosevelts lived here in Esopus and belonged to the militia. Incidentally, in those days we needed a militia to keep the marauders away. And today, 1940, we are trying to keep other marauders away from America." In both elections, he failed to carry Ulster County.

Three giant bronze statues, of Henry Hudson, Peter Stuyvesant, and George Clinton, loom over the west end of the green. J. Massey Rhind, a well-regarded American sculptor, created the three in 1898 for the Exchange Court, an office building at 52 Broadway in New York, where they stood on the cornice over the building entrances. In the 1940s the statues were removed and taken to a Brooklyn scrap yard, from which they were rescued by the philanthropy of Emily Crane Chadbourne (1871-1964) of Stone Ridge, president of the Senate House Association in 1935. A fourth statue, of British General and Anglo-Canadian hero James Wolfe, was also removed from Exchange Court and eventually found a home in Calgary. Chadbourne believed the three should come to Kingston as "memorials refreshing memories of generations to come" about their contributions to Kingston, New York, and the United States. Tradition holds that Stuyvesant negotiated a peace treaty with the Esopus Indians on this site. In 1950 the restored statues were brought to the park and placed on pedestals designed by a leading New York landscape architect, Alfred Geiffert, Jr. The granite pedestals were constructed by Byrne Brothers of Kingston, the firm that had erected the monument over Franklin Roosevelt's grave in Hyde Park. Queen Juliana of the Netherlands laid a wreath at the Stuyvesant statue in 1952 during the celebration of the city's 300th birthday.

Another rescued sculpture, a nineteenth-century, cast-iron urn-fountain made by J. W. Fiske Iron Works (New York) and given by the Children's Home of Kingston, was placed at the eastern end of Academy Green in 1982. It previously had stood on the grounds of St. Ursula's Academy on Grove Street.

4. EDWARD BRINK HOUSE
162 Clinton Avenue
c. 1865
Edward Brink

Although altered, this house is still interesting as the residence of Edward Brink, variously described as a "carpenter and architect" and "well known mechanic and architect." (Kingston *Journal*, June 13, 1867). The highly decorative porch, bracketed eaves, and especially the circular window high on the façade—a tiny version of the Gothic rose window—must have served to demonstrate Brink's talents. Brink had served as a carpen-

4. Edward Brink House

ter in the original construction (1850) of Minard Lafever's Old Dutch Church. Later, in 1861, he was the architect for the rebuilding of the church's steeple. In a stone plaque on the façade of the eight-room brick school built in 1871 on Green and Crown Streets, Brink is identified as architect. Originally School District No. 11, today the building serves as central administration for the Kingston Consolidated Schools. Brink's small tombstone in Wiltwyck Cemetery is simply inscribed "Edward Brink/Mar. 14, 1814/June 7, 1877."

5. JAMES B. WEEKS HOUSE
("The Columns")
26 Pearl Street
c. 1839

The best example of a Greek Revival house in Kingston, the Weeks house is fronted by four fluted Doric columns that support an entablature and pediment. The façade resem-

bles a small, ancient Greek temple and is suggestive of the high cultural aspirations of Americans in the 1830s and of their admiration of ancient Greeks as initiators of democracy. But in contrast to Greek classical practice, which demanded symmetry, the front door is placed off center to allow a commodious front parlor. The door itself is Greek-inspired in its anthemion ornament, radiating clusters of blossoms.

Andrew Jackson Downing, the Newburgh landscape gardener and nationally prominent architectural tastemaker of the mid-nineteenth century, favored Gothic and picturesque, irregular designs to the formality of the Greek Revival. In *Cottage Residences* (1842) he attacked the "false taste" of designing houses "in the form of Greek temples, sacrificing thereby the beauty of variety, much convenience, and all the comfort of low, shady verandas, to the ambitious display of a portico of stately columns." Downing would disapprove not only of the columnar portico, but also of the windows squeezed into the entabla-

5. James B. Weeks House

ture to light the cramped second floor of the Weeks house.

This is sometimes identified as the Hoes house. John C. F. Hoes purchased the house in 1867, and with his wife occupied it upon his retirement from Old Dutch Church. In the late nineteenth century, it was known as "The Columns."

Another Greek Revival house, the Christian F. Philips house (c. 1848-1853) at 120 St. James Street, has a four-column portico of the Ionic order.

6. ST. JAMES METHODIST EPISCOPAL CHURCH
Corner of Fair and Pearl Streets
1893
George W. Kramer (Werry and Kramer)

This is Kingston's best example of the Romanesque Revival, or more properly, the Richardsonian Romanesque of the great Boston architect, Henry Hobson Richardson,

as seen in his Trinity Church in Boston. Characteristic of Richardsonian Romanesque are the round arches, massive stone walls, brownstone trim of windows and doors, stubby columns with stylized leaf capitals by the doorway, reddish tile, and pyramidally-shaped tower roof. Where Richardson played the brownstone trim against light-colored granite walls, however, George Kramer used green stone from West Chester, Pennsylvania, for the broad wall surfaces. The color of the walls was heightened through the expansive stained glass windows lighting the sanctuary. Also in contrast to Richardson, Kramer angled the tower and entrance at its base to beckon people on both Fair and Pearl Streets. Those who entered found a sanctuary or auditorium laid out on the Akron plan, with an arc of pews facing the central pulpit and choir, and with folding doors allowing the joining of auditorium and Sunday school.

George W. Kramer (1847-1938) was a native of Akron, Ohio, where he practiced until 1894, when he opened an office in New York. He specialized in church designs, and

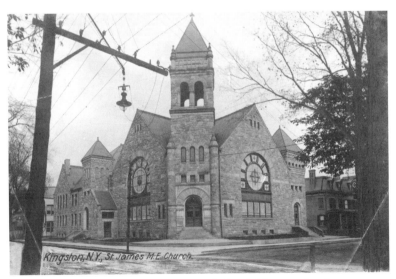

6. St. James Methodist Episcopal Church (vintage photo)

in 1897 published *The What and Why of Church Building*, including a photo of St. James. The First Baptist Church in Lakewood, New Jersey, closely resembles St. James.

7. SECOND REFORMED DUTCH CHURCH
(Fair Street Reformed Church)
219 Fair Street
1850
Thomas Thomas, Jr.

New York architect Thomas Thomas, Jr., designed the monumental, stone Second Reformed Dutch Church with Gothic Revival buttresses and pointed-arched windows and

doors surmounted by drip moldings. Originally the tower was topped with a fifty-foot wooden spire, but it fell in 1854. Early plans called for brick walls, but in the end, limestone from a quarry on upper Pearl Street was used. Original watercolor drawings for the design by Thomas are preserved by the church.

The choice of Gothic may have been a part of the congregation's declaration of independence from First, or Old Dutch Church, which, in 1850, was worshipping in a Greek Revival structure and would soon occupy a new Georgian or English Renaissance-style building. While details of Second Reformed Dutch Church are Gothic, the raised basement is not, and the symmetrical composition is still

7. Second Reformed Dutch Church (Thomas drawing)

classical. Further, it belongs to the tradition of Protestant hall churches; the boxy interior or "audience room" was designed for preaching, not elaborate and obscure ritual involving an altar in a recessed chancel of the sort preferred by stricter Gothic Revival architects like Richard Upjohn when designing Episcopal churches.

NYS and NR 2001

8. MYRON TELLER HOUSE
203 Fair Street at Maiden Lane
c. 1877

Adorned at the eaves with Italianate brackets enriched with leaf patterns, the Teller house catches the eye of the pedestrian, most particularly because of its similarly ornamented oriel or second-story bay window hovering

8. Myron Teller House

above Maiden Lane. It was a bay window such as this that moved the *Daily Freeman* (August 7, 1874) to describe "a new architectural fancy," the "rage uptown" for bay windows. "No man of property can consider himself in style unless a bay window has been added to the house." Upper-story bay windows were said to be especially fashionable as a sign of wealth, and looked well when "studded with flowers" or, even better, "an attractive lady." In the late nineteenth and early twentieth centuries, this house was occu-

pied by Myron Teller (not the architect, but a businessman involved with tanning, steamboats, coal, and lumber).

9. VAN BUREN-GORDON HOUSE
28 Green Street at Maiden Lane
Eighteenth century

This story-and-a-half, gable-roofed stone house was burned by the British in 1777 and rebuilt soon thereafter. The use of brick in the present end gables is an example of the mixing of stone walls with brick or wooden gables that is common in early Hudson Valley houses. Architectural historian Neil Larson suggests that the doorway and the small second-story windows were modifications made in the early nineteenth century.

Helen Wilkinson Reynolds noted that the Van Buren house had been restored by Myron Teller. She recommended Teller as a restoration architect who belonged to the Holland Society, and so was proud of his old Dutch ancestry. Moreover, he was "possessed of specialized architectural knowledge of the stone houses of Ulster County." His restoration of the Van Buren House, carried out in 1920 for Mrs. Mae K. Gordon, was "an illustration of the possibilities latent in many old dwellings for the creation of artistic, modern homes."

HLPC

9. Van Buren-Gordon House

10. FIRST CHURCH OF CHRIST SCIENTIST
161 Fair Street
1914
George W. Anderson

The classical architecture of First Church of Christ Scientist does not resemble other churches of its time in the city, and this may be understood as an expression of its isolation from those churches. In 1914, Protestant clergy in Kingston publicly decried Christian Science as "un-Christian and unscientific" and "a pestiferous nuisance." Designers of Christian Science churches early in the twentieth century generally avoided the Gothic Revival style, popular with other churches. The Gothic was thought to be a style joined to gloom, mystery, and superstition. Classical designs, on the other hand, seemed rational, cheerful, filled with light unfiltered by stained glass and free of medieval symbolism. This façade looks back to the Greek Revival of the 1830s and 1840s: two Ionic columns are placed next to squared piers or antae, all of which support an entablature and pediment. The fanlight in the pediment adds a touch of the Georgian, and the design as a whole was called "Colonial style" in 1914—at the time no distinction was made between architecture from the colonial era and the Greek Revival of the nineteenth century. The triangular windowpanes may have been considered churchly without being specifically Gothic.

10. First Church of Christ Scientist

11. Tobias Van Steenburgh House (vintage photo)

George W. Anderson, a member of the church, was engaged in real estate and sold the lot at 161 Fair Street to the church. He also is described in contemporary accounts as the "architect and builder" of the church, although city directories do not list him as an architect.

11. TOBIAS VAN STEENBURGH HOUSE
97 Wall Street at Franklin Street
Eighteenth century

A tablet placed on the front wall of this house in 1897 by the Wiltwyck Chapter of the D.A.R. identifies it as the residence of the Van Steenburgh family for two centuries, and, in agreement with many nineteenth-century historical accounts, cites it as Kingston's only house uninjured by the British when they burned the town in 1777.

The fieldstone, story-and-a-half house has a symmetrical arrangement of front door (with rectangular transom) and two windows on either side of the door, which suggests a post-1750 date of construction. An engraving in Schoonmaker's *History* (1888) shows no central gable, but two shed-roofed dormers, a porch roof cantilevered over the front door, and a stoop at its base. An early-twentieth-century photo records a now-replaced Gothic Revival window in the central gable, but neither of the dormers that now flank this gable. The wooden wings also date from the twentieth century. NYS and NR 1999; HLPC

12. HOME FOR THE AGED OF ULSTER COUNTY
(Hudson Valley Senior Residence)
80 Washington Avenue
1929-1930
George E. Lowe

Incorporated in 1919, this home was not a county institution for the indigent, but a private charity whose residence was intended

12. Home for the Aged of Ulster County

fresh air resulted in the many-windowed sun parlor and open second-story porch on the north and south sides.

13. BOULEVARD GULF SERVICE STATION (Cake Box Bakery and Café) Fair Street at Greenkill Avenue c. 1939

to appeal to women and men who had long functioned as responsible citizens. Its Georgian Revival façade, dominated by a pilastered portico, resembled mansions of the era and spoke of the high respectability of the institution and its residents. The seventeen elderly women who were the first residents could enjoy the elegantly paneled foyer, sitting rooms, and library. Theories of the time about the healthful benefits of sunlight and

By 1939, modernism, the rejection of the historic styles and the embracing of the simple, boxy volumes of the International Style, began to appear in the city's architectural landscape. Gas stations, as key elements in the twentieth-century auto revolution, were logical sites for the application of modernism. In the 1920s, however, architects like Teller and Halverson saw no contradiction in cloaking gas stations in seventeenth or eighteenth-century forms, as they did in a design for A. R. Newcombe Oil Corp. In the 1930s, some

13. Boulevard Gulf Service Station

3

14. M. A. Weishaupt Grocery

oil companies adorned the modern white box with distinctive forms so the customer, even when on an unfamiliar road, could identify the brand at a glance. Texaco, for example, had its red stars and three green horizontal bands, implying speed, on the upper wall.

This gas station resembled many in the mid-twentieth century in its surface of steel sheets coated with white porcelain enamel, and in the three speed bands running above windows and doors. But the blocky tower, with upper level fitted with recessed panels of glass blocks, defined the building as a Gulf station. Originally these panels glowed at night, illuminated from within, and "GULF" also appeared radiant near the top of the tower. The excitement of driving or riding in a fast car at night must have been enhanced by the visual drama of a fueling stop here.

After years of decline, the station's conversion just before the turn of the twenty-first century into Bodacious Bagels (Henry Konover architect) came at a time when aging examples

of modern roadside architecture (diners, gas stations, motels) had achieved the status of icons of American culture.

14. M. A. WEISHAUPT GROCERY (Charles Grocery and Deli) 229 Greenkill Avenue c. 1932

This building blends into the urban landscape, but at the same time it is an unusually well-preserved example of the neighborhood grocery store popular between the world wars. The completely unornamented, clapboarded, hipped-roofed, two-story, rectangular box of a building resembles many houses of the period. Here, however, the ground story front is fitted with plate-glass display windows and recessed entrance to the grocery, with a side entrance to the upper living quarters—all sheltered by a slightly projecting pent roof.

Albany Avenue in the early twentieth century.

TOUR 4:
ALBANY AVENUE DISTRICT

I n 1874 Albany Avenue was described as "becoming one of the choicest places for erecting dwelling houses in the city. It is extremely select, and the market value of the lots are of such a price, none but those who are well-off in this world's goods can afford to buy them." Lots on the north side of the avenue were quoted at $75 to $80 a foot, with $45 to $50 a foot for lots on the south side. (*Freeman*, November 12, 1874)

The avenue's reputation was at least as exalted in 1896 when R. Lionel DeLisser called it "one of the finest streets in Kingston. . . . The avenue is broad, with tall trees, that arching, show many a pretty vista of lawn and street, and shade the handsome residences which occupy its either side." (DeLisser, *Picturesque Ulster*, p.36)

4

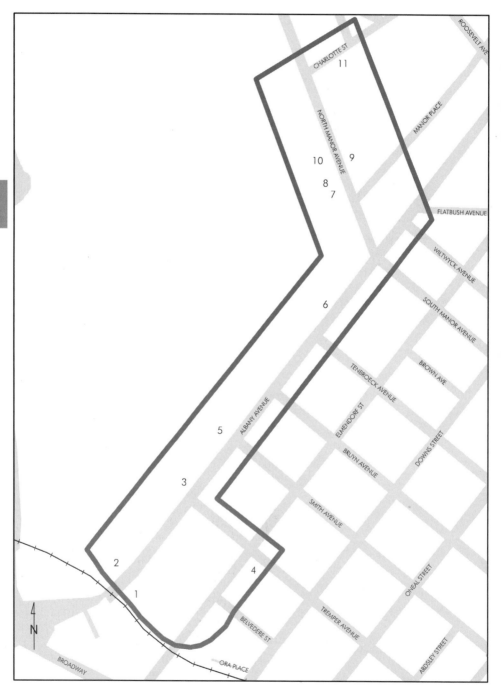

TOUR 4:
ALBANY AVENUE DISTRICT

1. SHARP BURYING GROUND
2. EMMA F. FREER HOUSE
3. ST. JOHN'S EPISCOPAL CHURCH
4. FIRST PRESBYTERIAN CHURCH
5. HENRY W. OTIS HOUSE
6. ERNEST STEUDING HOUSE
7. CHARLES L. AND ELLA M. ARNOLD HOUSE
8. JOHN L. AND A. JEANNETTE MACKINNON HOUSE
9. HALVERSON HOUSE
10. RALPH J. GREGORY HOUSE
11. GEORGE B. AND BARBARA H. MATTHEWS HOUSE

4

1. SHARP BURYING GROUND
148 Albany Avenue
1832

The plan of this "burying ground" was drawn in pen and ink by Edward O'Neil on September 20, 1832, and is preserved at the Ulster County Historical Society's Bevier House in Marbletown. It delineates 210 burial lots on a regular grid aligned with Albany Avenue, then "Albany Road." The picturesquely designed rural cemetery with informal, park-like landscaping, such as the ones at Montrepose and Wiltwyck, was some twenty years away.

John Sudam (1782-1835), whose Federal-style house stands at Wall and Main Streets, is buried here in a family plot. In 1880 historian Nathaniel Bartlett Sylvester, author of *History of Ulster County, New York*, singled out the O'Neil family lot as "large and handsome." Today the monument of the planner of the burying ground, Edward O'Neil (born in Ireland 1785, died in

Kingston 1856, and a founder of the Methodist Episcopal Church in Kingston in 1830), remains impressive, as does the obelisk over the grave of Abraham Hasbrouck (1773-1845). In the 1832 plan, the parsonages of the Baptist, Dutch, and Methodist churches are each identified as owning two of the 16.5-by-20-foot lots closest to the Albany Road. This would indicate that the cemetery of Old Dutch church was either full or considered unsanitary, and that some sort of peace reigned in the Protestant ranks.

Sylvester wrote in 1880 that the "plat is very handsome, and worthy of better care than appears now to be given to it." He found that "many of the remains have evidently been removed"—probably for reburial at Wiltwyck or Montrepose. In the late twentieth century the grounds again looked neglected, but in 1995 the Friends of Historic Kingston presented a new fence by Hurley blacksmith Ron Rifenburg, and undertook other improvements.

1. Sharp Burying Ground

2. EMMA F. FREER HOUSE
151 Albany Avenue
c. 1896-1898
Wilson Eyre

This Colonial Revival house (called a "cottage" when new) was designed by Wilson Eyre of Philadelphia, one of America's foremost architects of the period, and appeared in leading architectural periodicals. Emma Freer's house represents the move towards order in the 1890s after the livelier, asymmetrical compositions of the Queen Anne as seen in the Dr. Elbert Loughran house on Main Street. Still, Eyre could not quite bring himself to design a completely symmetrical Georgian façade. The wooden quoins refer back to Georgian sources. The pent roof between the first and second stories is a feature of colonial architecture near Philadelphia, and not indigenous to Ulster County.

Floor plans by Eyre dated August 25, 1896, indicate that he oriented the dining room, living room, and library on the first floor, and three bedrooms on the second floor, to the western view and away from the bustle of Albany Avenue. The first floor kitchen and second-story bathrooms faced Albany Avenue.

In 1890, Emma Freer's brother, Charles Lang Freer, a Kingston native, wealthy builder of railroad freight cars in Detroit, and noted art collector, commissioned Eyre to design his Detroit residence. Quarries near Kingston provided bluestone for this house, and the Kingston firm of Darling Bros. and Burger sent its masons to Detroit to build the house. Eyre also sketched a "Proposed Cottage for Mr. Freer at Kingston, N.Y." Probably not built, it was to be a modest, story-and-a-half cottage of clapboards with a "Dutch Colonial" gambrel roof.

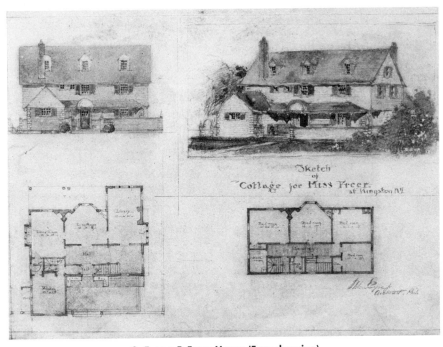

2. Emma F. Freer House (Eyre drawing)

3. ST. JOHN'S EPISCOPAL CHURCH
207 Albany Avenue
1835, 1861, 1926

St. John's Church was founded in 1832 and originally located on Wall Street. About 1834 Edward J. Webb, a New York architect, made a rendering of the church's side elevation in the Greek Revival style. Talbot Hamlin saw the drawing in the Senate House Museum and wrote admiringly about it in his *Greek Revival Architecture in America* (1944); the drawing cannot now be located. The building consecrated in 1835 was enlarged in 1861. At that time it probably received its medieval revival façade, built according to a plan furnished by George W.

Pratt, a businessman and a founder of the Ulster County Historical Society in 1859, who, as Colonel Pratt, died of a wound received at the Second Battle of Manassas, Virginia, in 1862.

In 1926 the Reade Theater chain offered $100,000 for the land on which the church stood at 319 Wall Street. The stone walls were taken down and the façade re-erected in front of a new, wider structure (George E. Lowe, architect) in the prestigious residential district of Albany Avenue, a marked contrast from the tightly built-up Wall Street commercial district.

The church's façade is graced on the southeast corner by a well-designed tower and spire of Gothic Revival proportions,

3. St. John's Episcopal Church (vintage photo)

although the arches are semicircular or Romanesque throughout the fortress-like façade. The real glory of the church is to be found within, because of its rich stained glass and woodcarvings. Some of the woodcarvings were executed by George Huber; the wooden pulpit and litany desk were designed by Percy Fowler and carved by Edward Maene (1852-1931), a Philadelphia craftsman trained in Belgium and Paris. The rectory behind the church is an old stone house (thought by some to have been the Thomas Chambers Manor House) restored by Teller and Halverson in 1940.
HLPC

4. FIRST PRESBYTERIAN CHURCH
80 Elmendorf Street
1878
J. A. Wood

Although Kingston native Charles Romeyn submitted plans for a new First Presbyterian Church in 1877, it was J. A. Wood whose design was ultimately chosen in 1878. A decade earlier he had completed a Gothic Revival building of bluestone, with reddish brown stone trim, for First Baptist Church on Albany Avenue. Its broad, low nave was in contrast to a tower with spire and pinnacles, vertical accents that drew attention to the main entrance, even though the tower entrance was set back from the avenue. (The pinnacles distributed over the exterior are gone, and the Albany Avenue façade has been altered.)

For First Presbyterian, constructed of brick with stone trim, Wood brought the tower forward to the corner of Elmendorf Street and Tremper Avenue where it, too, served to draw attention to a main entrance. The *Kingston Press* (January 30, 1868) had criticized the low pitch of the First Baptist roof as un-Gothic; First

Presbyterian's roof has a steeper pitch. Both churches are hall churches, with a unified interior space and central pulpit intended to promote the role of the preacher. Wood's use of the Gothic Revival for Baptist and Presbyterian churches went against the preference of Richard Upjohn, the most famous church architect of the mid-nineteenth century and a High Church Episcopalian, for limiting the Gothic to congregations whose rituals approximated those of England before the Reformation.

4. First Presbyterian Church

5. HENRY W. OTIS HOUSE
231 Albany Avenue
1875
Henry W. Otis, builder

Perhaps Kingston's finest surviving Second Empire-style, mansard-roofed house is the Otis house, clearly intended to be a

5. Henry W. Otis House

showplace on newly-fashionable Albany Avenue. Henry Otis (1843-1928) was the city's leading builder in the 1870s; the *Daily Freeman,* (July 24, 1873) observed that he was the busiest man in town, routinely carrying "two or three embryo buildings in his coat pocket." He executed several designs, including the Alms House and Armory, conceived by J. A. Wood, the Mid-Hudson's foremost architect of the period and possibly the designer of the Otis house.

In his early thirties when he finished building his own residence, Otis opened the "fine . . . mansion" to the public before occupying it (*Kingston Daily Freeman*, August 13, 1875), evidence of his talent for self-promo-

tion. The strikingly tall, tower-like mansard at the corner is fitted with a variation of the three-part Palladian window; above are two port-hole windows. The iron cresting atop the roof, polychrome brick and stone walls, and vigor-ously detailed brackets and porch posts, all add to the sense of a house asserting its pres-ence on the avenue.
HLPC

6. ERNEST STEUDING HOUSE
309 Albany Avenue
c. 1912

Labeled a "fine Kingston home" in a series of original photo postcards by Woodstock photographer Louis E. Jones pro-duced in the early twentieth century, the Steuding house is representative of the pro-gressive spirit in early-twentieth-century archi-tecture, as it cannot be categorized as belong-ing to one or another of the revival styles. Rather, its austere stucco walls, horizontal groupings of windows, and broadly sheltering green tile roof connect it to the Arts and Crafts movement. The great, hipped roof and its small eyebrow window do, however, hark back to the late nineteenth century and H. H. Richardson.

**6. Ernest Steuding House
(vintage photo)**

7. CHARLES L. AND ELLA M. ARNOLD HOUSE
175 North Manor Avenue
1937-1938
Charles S. Keefe

7. Charles L. and Ella M. Arnold House

Keefe described the Arnold house as "Tudor" style, although it has much in com-mon with his simple, gable-roofed Colonial Revival houses. Probably, the combination of dark stone walls and casement windows sig-nified Tudor to him. Indicative of the 1930s are the choice of steel for the casement frames and a veneer of stone for the walls. Charles Arnold was an officer of F. B. Matthews and Co., wholesale grocers, as was his neighbor, George Matthews, of 16 Charlotte Street.

Earlier, in 1936, Keefe had designed 215 North Manor Avenue, a "federal-colonial style" house with a stone-veneer façade, for Francis E. O'Connor, a physician, and his wife Natalita. T. I. Rifenbary and Son (Jay W. Rifenbary) was the contractor for both the Arnold and O'Connor houses; Jay Rifenbary's shop and home were not far away, at 379 Albany Avenue.

Still earlier, the important New York architectural firm of Albro and Lindeberg had designed the F. G. Schmidt house (1909) in the

Old English style near the northern end of Manor Avenue. An old stone house on the site had been demolished to provide a place for the new stucco and half-timbered structure, whose plan rambled to avoid admired elm trees. A critic, in a 1911 issue of *Country Life in America,* thought the low house rested among the elms "as comfortably as though it had stood there for generations."

8. JOHN L. AND A. JEANNETTE MACKINNON HOUSE
181 North Manor Avenue
1934-1935
Teller and Halverson

The MacKinnon house received national attention when it was selected by *House Beautiful* in 1935 to be part of an exhibition of photos traveling to department stores. Harry Halverson was responsible for the design, and he and his wife Marion joined the MacKinnons in attending the opening of the exhibition at Macy's in New York. Halverson in 1984 referred to the MacKinnon house as his "favorite" among his residential designs. Myron Teller provided the hand-wrought iron hardware that adorns the house.

8. John L. and A. Jeannette MacKinnon House

Although not a small house, its colonial style is unpretentious. It has the appearance of a spacious cottage that has grown over time, as the façade of the main block is surfaced with boards nailed flush to the frame, while the two "additions" are clapboarded. The "additions" were actually built simultaneously with the main block. The northwestern "addition" was originally the garage, whose function was disguised on the Manor Avenue front. John MacKinnon was a Kingston chiropractor.

9. HALVERSON HOUSE
186 North Manor Avenue
1924
Harry Halverson

9. Halverson House with Harry Halverson, 1984

As a young architect recently graduated from Syracuse University's College of

Architecture, Harry Halverson designed this unpretentious Colonial Revival house for his parents, Louis and Aldina Carina Olson Halverson. Louis was a Kingston contractor and builder. The story-and-a-half house, with gable roof curving out over the front and a simple stoop at the doorway, was probably considered Dutch Colonial, but without the effort at following regional Dutch precedent in stone that would mark the better-known houses Halverson did later, in partnership with Myron Teller. By 1931 Harry Halverson and his wife Marion resided here, and he died in the house in 1988, at age ninety-six.

10. RALPH J. GREGORY HOUSE
189 North Manor Avenue
c. 1910 and later
Gerard W. Betz

10. Ralph J. Gregory House

The original portion of this house—that to the north—was designed as a substantial bungalow by Gerard W. Betz about 1910 for Ralph J. Gregory. The section to the south, with steeper gable roof, was a later addition. The stucco walls, low-pitched gable roof with broad dormer, and simple but sturdy details of the original section relate it to the Arts and

Crafts movement in architecture and the decorative arts. Appropriately, Gregory & Co., of which Ralph Gregory was vice president, sold Arts and Crafts furniture at 661 Broadway. In 1916 they were agents for "Limbert's Hand-Made Furniture," a rival of Gustav Stickley's better-known Craftsman enterprise.

11. GEORGE B. AND BARBARA H. MATTHEWS HOUSE
16 Charlotte Street
1937-1938
Teller and Halverson

Here, Teller and Halverson drew upon their knowledge of the regional Dutch colonial. The Matthews house resembles a one-and-a-half-story, Dutch fieldstone house with wood gable end and later wooden addition to the north. While partially of stone, it also resembles the partners' MacKinnon house nearby on North Manor Avenue, down to the finely proportioned doorway with sidelights. George Matthews was an official in F. B. Matthews and Co., wholesale grocers.

11. George B. and Barbara H. Matthews House

City hall and horse-drawn streetcar on Union Avenue, now Broadway.
(lithograph, *County Atlas of Ulster,* 1875)

TOUR 5:
BROADWAY

Union Avenue joined the former villages of Kingston and Rondout until 1893, when its name was changed to Broadway, much to the consternation of some merchants who thought it was too narrow, especially downtown in Rondout, to be so named. They feared Kingston would be accused of "aping our betters." (*Freeman*, August 19, 1893) At the same time electric trolleys began running on Broadway. The *Freeman* (August 9, 1893) editorialized that the greater speed of the trolleys, in comparison with the old horse cars, and a five-cent fare would work to diminish "clannishness and unreasoning jealousy" between Kingston and Rondout. "Kingston will henceforth be a real city instead of an aggregation of villages under a municipal government. There will be a constant increase in the number of men who do business in one end of the town and reside in the other."

City hall was built to house the new city government created in 1872 by unifying the villages of Kingston and Rondout, and rises from the boundary which once divided them. Broadway near city hall became the civic center of Kingston with the eventual construction of the armory, hospital, library and high school.

5

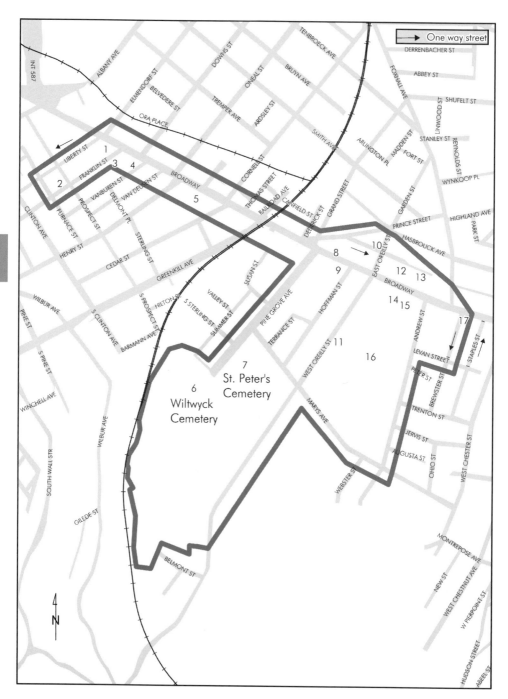

TOUR 5:
BROADWAY

1. **ROBERT G. BONESTEEL HOUSE**
2. **DISTRICT SCHOOL NO. 8**
   (Kingston Library)
3. **AFRICAN METHODIST EPISCOPAL ZION CHURCH**
4. **GREGORY & BARNES FURNITURE**
   (Earl B. Feiden, Inc.)
5. **BROADWAY THEATRE**
   (Ulster Performing Arts Center)
6. **WILTWYCK RURAL CEMETERY**
7. **ST. PETER'S CEMETERY**
8. **HUTTON BUILDING**
9. **NEW YORK STATE ARMORY**
   (Midtown Neighborhood Center)
10. **CENTRAL FIRE STATION, MUNICIPAL BUILDING**
11. **LASHER HOUSE**
12. **KINGSTON CITY HALL**
13. **KINGSTON CITY LABORATORY, ULSTER COUNTY TUMOR CLINIC**
14. **KINGSTON HIGH SCHOOL**
15. **KINGSTON CITY LIBRARY**
   (Kingston City Schools Consolidated)
16. **MYRON J. MICHAEL JUNIOR HIGH SCHOOL**
   (Kingston High School Campus)
17. **J. J. AND FRANK W. ALBRECHT GROCERY**
   (Arace Electronics)

5

1. ROBERT G. BONESTEEL HOUSE
693 Broadway
c. 1866

Although much altered, the distinctive octagonal plan of the Bonesteel house proclaims it a survivor of the octagon house fad initiated by Orson Squire Fowler with his book, *A Home for All; or the Gravel Wall, and Octagon Mode of Building* (1848 and 1853). Fowler, an ardent reformer and phrenologist, preached the benefits of the octagonal house plan, claiming it enclosed more space than a conventional rectangular plan given the same exterior wall dimensions, and that housewives would walk fewer steps as they performed their chores. Fowler's own octagonal house (1853) near Fishkill was built with gravel or concrete walls, but the Kingston example is of brick and bluestone, both probably from local sources. Like many octagonal houses, the eaves are supported with Italianate brackets; here the angles of the octagon are marked by brick pilasters. By 1887 and probably from the outset, a wooden porch wrapped around three sides facing Broadway (then Union Avenue).

The 1870 Beers map of Kingston and Rondout represents the octagonal plan of the house and identifies it as Robert G. Bonesteel's. Bonesteel, an ice dealer, died in November 1869. The family monument in Wiltwyck Cemetery is a handsome obelisk shrouded with tasseled drapery in marble.

2. DISTRICT SCHOOL NO. 8
(Kingston Library)
55 Franklin Street
1878, 1888
W. W. Goodrich, Andrew Mason

The present polychrome, bracketed, Italianate-style building replaced a Gothic Revival school on the site pictured in the 1875 county atlas. A plaque over the doorway of the western portion of former District School No. 8 confirms that W. W. Goodrich was the architect of the 1878 structure. Henry W. Otis was the mason: the brick walls have stone accents at the corners, foundation line, and in the segmental-arched windows. A wooden octagonal cupola once stood above the western entrance.

2. District School No. 8 (vintage photo)

The larger eastern part of the building was designed by Andrew Mason in 1888, as is indicated on a plaque on the eastern façade. Mason continued Goodrich's Italianate design, but announced the presence of metal piers within the north and south brick walls. He did so by affixing iron oval panels

1. Robert G. Bonesteel House

3. African Methodist Episcopal Zion Church

to the exterior walls and bolting these panels through the brick to the metal piers, one of which is visible in the library's reference room. The Kingston Library departed its cramped, but distinguished, classical building on Broadway for this capacious building converted to library uses in 1978.

3. AFRICAN METHODIST EPISCOPAL ZION CHURCH
26 Franklin Street
1927-1930
Thomas P. Rice

The combination of round-arched Romanesque and pointed-arched Gothic found on the front of the A. M. E. Zion Church was widely adopted by Christian congregations, regardless of race, in the early

1900s. So, too, was the raising of the main sanctuary over the partially-below-ground Sunday school.

This congregation had played a key role in Kingston's Black community for seventy-nine years when the cornerstone of its present building was laid in 1927. About 1924, the Rev. Ebenezer O. Clarke, pastor of the church, began discussions with architect Thomas Rice about replacing the existing building with one that would provide both religious and recreational facilities. Rev. Clarke believed (according to the *Daily Freeman*, January 28, 1926) that "as there could be no unification between his people and the people of other churches of the city, it was very necessary that the negro people of the city have a distinct building to worship in." White business and civic leaders, including Judges G. D. B. Hasbrouck and A. T.

5

Clearwater, were instrumental in raising funds for construction; the White community was troubled that young Blacks "have become disassociated from the restraining and elevating influences of religious life." (*Freeman*, March 9, 1927) Rice announced that he would donate his professional services. Memorials included a baptismal font given in memory of General George Sharpe.

4. GREGORY & BARNES FURNITURE
(Earl B. Feiden, Inc.)
661-663 Broadway
c. 1899

A ghostly sign on the west wall still recalls the furniture company that originally occupied this well-designed and preserved four-story commercial building a century ago. Indicative of taste around 1900 are the light, tawny-colored bricks, Renaissance cornice, and pilasters that help unify the upper three stories and suggest the upward thrust of an embryonic skyscraper. Cast-iron piers and Italianate details were now *passe*. The big show windows on Broadway once displayed household furnishings, including the well-designed and constructed Arts and Crafts products of Charles P. Limbert.

4. Gregory & Barnes Furniture

5. Broadway Theatre (vintage photo)

5. BROADWAY THEATRE
(Ulster Performing Arts Center)
601 Broadway
1926-1927
Douglass Hall with George E. Lowe

The Broadway Theatre at Ulster Performing Arts Center is one of Kingston's few remaining historic theatres. The main entrance, currently distinguished by a giant Corinthian porch, was originally a severe, classical pavilion made eye-catching with an electrically illuminated marquee and vertical sign. Marquee and sign were removed in the 1950s—the latter is echoed by the surviving Mohican Market sign. Stores have always been located on either side of the theatre entrance and behind stripped, classical walls accented with colorful tiles.

The interior is much more exuberantly ornamented, with classical forms intended to simulate the romantic aura of Spain. On opening night, June 9, 1927, the *Freeman* observed that "in carrying out the Spanish note in the decorations the ushers, who are girls, were gowned in Spanish costumes." Managing Director Harry Lazarus succeeded in bringing his audience to roar with laughter at the feature (silent) film, *Cradle Snatchers*. They also enjoyed "five sets of first class vaudeville," a "six girl jazz band," the Broadway Theatre Orchestra, and organist Thomas Crosby.

Douglass Hall was a New York architect who specialized in theatre design. His Broadway Theatre was said to duplicate a theatre recently completed in Port Chester. George Lowe was the local architect who supervised construction.
NYS and NR 1979

5

6. Wiltwyck Rural Cemetery

6. WILTWYCK RURAL CEMETERY
145 Pine Grove Avenue
1850 and later

The picturesque cemetery on the fringe of the city was mid-nineteenth-century America's solution to the problem of overcrowded and unsanitary burial grounds in urban church-yards. Following the precedent of Mount Auburn Cemetery (planned in 1831) in Cambridge, Massachusetts, and Green-Wood Cemetery (opened in 1840) in Brooklyn, Wiltwyck was organized in 1850, reorga-

nized in 1856, and laid out as a romantic park with irregular drives carefully planned to flow with the naturally rolling contours of the land. Walks and burial plots, however, were planned according to a geometric grid within these irregular drives. In 1857 the cemetery advertised for lot purchasers, persons "who desire to make this beautiful Cemetery a source of pride and pleasure to the inhabitants of Kingston and their numerous visitors." At this time cemeteries like Wiltwyck functioned not just as burial grounds, but also as parks for quiet, contemplative strolls on a Sunday afternoon. Since the 1880s, such strolls have occasionally been interrupted by the passing of a West Shore train along the cemetery's western boundary.

The photo accompanying this entry shows the obelisk with draped urn marking the grave of Kingston builder Henry Otis (1843-1928). Perhaps the most noteworthy monument is that of John Vanderlyn (1775-1852), the Kingston native and neoclassical artist whose work attracted the attention of French Emperor Napoleon I, but who died poor in Kingston. His monument was not erected until about 1892. Nearby is a classical monument over the grave of Sara Elizabeth Downs Smith, a young woman whose portrait Vanderlyn painted. A section of the cemetery is devoted to Jewish burials. The mortuary (1929) is a weighty rectangular block with entrance dignified by a pair of Greek Doric columns and pediment.

World War II Congressional Medal of Honor winner Robert H. Dietz (1921-1945) is buried beneath a monument (1949) designed by Robert Winchell of Byrne Brothers, monument dealers at 635 Broadway. The basic shape of the Vermont granite monument was inspired by Hudson Valley colonial headstones. The carved ornament was enriched with a band of laurel and the design of the Medal of Honor, as well as the signature of Harry S. Truman below an excerpt from the citation describing Dietz's heroism. Byrne Brothers also erected the monument over Franklin Roosevelt's grave in Hyde Park.

7. ST. PETER'S CEMETERY
110 Pine Grove Avenue
c. 1870 and later

St. Peter's Cemetery was established by Father Kuhnen after 1887 as the German Roman Catholic cemetery of the city, although the 1870 Beers map of Kingston and Rondout

marks the site as an unnamed cemetery. St. Peter's Cemetery lies adjacent to, but separated from, the more wooded and park-like Wiltwyck Cemetery, which in 1899 was described as "Protestant," although there was a section for Jews. A number of the monument inscriptions in St. Peter's are in German. Among the most prominent memorials are the mausoleum of Jacob Rice (1847-1930), a boat builder on Abeel Street, and the Barmann monument. Peter Barmann (1844-1908) was a brewer on Greenkill Avenue.

7. St. Peter's Cemetery

8. HUTTON BUILDING
478 Broadway
1906

The name "Hutton," worked out in relief in the brick panel of the arched parapet atop 478 Broadway, links this building to the brick-manufacturing family; Lester Hutton and Robert K. Hutton were the original owners of the building and were engaged in brick mak-

ing and real estate through The Hutton Company. The building's brick walls are relieved by bluestone bands and keystones around the oval attic windows. The broad second-story oriel projects over the street-level entrance to, originally, William J. Rifenburg's restaurant, and later to a succession of pharmacies during whose occupancy the entrance front was sleekly modernized.

8. Hutton Building

9. New York State Armory (vintage photo)

9. NEW YORK STATE ARMORY
(Midtown Neighborhood Center)
467 Broadway
1878-1879
J. A. Wood

The armory's octagonal tower with crenellated battlements, and the narrow, slit windows in the tower and adjoining walls, were meant to resemble a medieval castle. While some critics have likened late-nineteenth-century armories to fairy tale castles, in fact they were designed with very serious purposes in mind. Here, the 75-by-150-foot drill room provided space to train the militia, and the walls were strong enough to be defended against unruly mobs. The 1870s were a time of labor unrest throughout the country, including Kingston. In 1876, for example, following layoffs of Ulster and Delaware Railroad workers, arsonists destroyed the railroad shops.

The site of the armory—originally to be built with county funds—was chosen in 1875 for its proximity to city hall, and at that time a plan by Arthur Crooks, city hall's architect, was chosen. Construction was delayed by the economic depression of the mid-1870s and by strong opposition to the use of local public funds after the considerable expenditure for city hall. State funds were finally used in 1878-1879, and Wood replaced Crooks. In 1879 Wood designed the armory in Newburgh with a similar vocabulary of castle forms. In 1933-1934 the Kingston armory was enlarged and remodeled by Teller and Halverson, with the help of funds from FDR's New Deal, to serve as the Municipal Auditorium. A new National Guard armory had been erected in 1931 on Kiersted Avenue at Manor Avenue. Its architect was the young Albert Edward Milliken.
HLPC

10. CENTRAL FIRE STATION
19 East O'Reilly Street
1908
Myron S. Teller

MUNICIPAL BUILDING
23-25 East O'Reilly Street
1911
Thomas P. Rice

The scale of these two buildings and their proximity to city hall suggest the growth of municipal government and its effort to centralize services to meet the needs of the twentieth-century city. A paid fire department was organized in 1907, apparently in response to refusals by insurance companies to insure property in the city. Teller's design is a late and geometricized version of the bracketed Italianate with small polychrome touches. A hose-drying tower rises from the fire station; early photos show it with horse-drawn equipment and three, arched equipment doorways later made wider and rectangular. Although Teller is not credited with the design of the Municipal Building, it closely resembles his fire station.

The fire station's interior and apparatus were described for the public in 1909: "On the ground floor is situated the stalls and spaces for the horses of the department. There is the Weiner hose wagon, the Wiltwyck hook and ladder, the chief's wagon and old steamer Lackawanna. The stalls are situated advantageously for quick hitching to the trucks and all harness is equipped with attachments to be released at the stroke of the alarm. The doors opening on to the street are also connected in like manner. . . .

"On the second floor are located the chief's office, a light airy room, with bath and toilet near by. The dormitories for members of the company are also located on this floor, as are also the pool room, two club rooms and two baths. A locker room is conveniently located to the sleeping rooms. The brass sliding poles leading to the ground floor are also located in the dormitories." (*Freeman*, March 10, 1909)

10. Central Fire Station (vintage photo)

11. LASHER HOUSE
66 West O'Reilly Street
c. 1928

This is a fine specimen of the inexpensive, early-twentieth-century bungalow, a low, story-and-a-half house whose broad, gently pitched gable roof has a wide dormer and extends to encompass front and back porches. The stuccoed walls, angular bay window, and chunky porch posts refer to no historical style. This mildly progressive house type had wide appeal for practical-minded middle-class and skilled working-class families. This house was first occupied by Claude and Mary Lasher; he was an engineer on the Ulster and Delaware Railroad. A similar, but smaller, bungalow can be seen at the corner of Flatbush and Tietjen Avenues.

11. Lasher House

12. KINGSTON CITY HALL
420 Broadway
1873-1875
Arthur Crooks
Alterations by George E. Lowe, Gerard W. Betz, and Myron S. Teller, 1927-1928
Restored by John G. Waite Associates, 1998-2000

Built as a symbol of the vigor of the new City of Kingston formed from the villages of Kingston and Rondout, Kingston City Hall stands on the border once dividing the villages. The central tower rises boldly and suggests civic pride and authority, as does the tower of city hall's medieval source, the fortified Palazzo Vecchio, or town hall, of Florence. Before winning the competition for city hall in 1873, Arthur Crooks had worked as a draftsman in the New York office of Richard Upjohn, the country's leading designer of Gothic Revival churches. Among the runners-up in the competition was William Appleton Potter, who would go on to a distinguished career in planning Romanesque and Gothic Revival churches. As originally designed by Crooks, city hall's walls and arches were boldly polychromatic in brick and stone in accord with the Gothic taste of John Ruskin, the English critic. St. Peter's Roman Catholic Church in Rosendale, completed by Crooks in 1876, is a well-preserved example of his Ruskinian Gothic designs.

A fire gutted the interior in 1927 and resulted in extensive alterations to the exterior that reflected the 1920s preference for simplicity and dislike of Victorian exuberance. In 1972 the city government departed the building, but, after years of neglect, city hall was magnificently restored during the administration of the late mayor, T. R. Gallo, and was reopened as the center of municipal government in 2000.

The lawn before city hall is the site of several patriotic monuments to those from Ulster County who have served the United States in wartime since the Civil War. The most imposing monument, dedicated "to the soldiers and sailors of the County of Ulster in the war for the Union, 1861-1865," is dominated by a marble, classically-garbed figure representing Liberty. Below her are realistic figures in bronze portraying a Union soldier and sailor, sculpted in 1890 by Casper Buberl

5

(1834-1899). Civil War veteran, landscape painter, and Rondout citizen, Jervis McEntee, was a member of the committee that oversaw the creation of the monument in 1889. During the war, McEntee had erected a flagpole at his studio-residence as a sign of his devotion to the Union cause. General George H. Sharpe also played a leading role in selecting the design.

The World War I memorial, with reliefs of a soldier and sailor by James Edward Kelly, was commissioned in 1918 shortly before the end of the war. Funds were raised from "industrial workers."
NYS and NR 1971

13. KINGSTON CITY LABORATORY
400 Broadway
1935-1940
Teller and Halverson

12. Kingston City Hall

13. Kingston City Laboratory and Ulster County Tumor Clinic (Teller and Halverson drawing)

ULSTER COUNTY TUMOR CLINIC
400 Broadway
1947-1949
Harry Halverson

During its first half-century, Kingston Hospital and related medical facilities on Broadway were quartered in a number of Colonial Revival structures. The original building of the City of Kingston Hospital (1892-1894) was designed by Charles W. Romeyn, a Kingston native and successful New York architect. Its centerpiece was a cupolaed, gambrel-roofed building "in the old colonial style" that burned in 1926. George E. Lowe soon designed Georgian Revival blocks on Broadway that were made nearly invisible by new construction in the 1980s.

The Ulster County Tumor Clinic and the earlier City Laboratory, which had been erected in two stages with the aid of the Federal Work Projects Administration, were demolished in 2002, as this guide was in preparation. Although erected a dozen years apart, both buildings, designed mainly by Harry

Halverson, had red-brick walls and modest, white Georgian trim. They were attempts to create tasteful, quiet, and reassuringly home-like settings for the diagnosis and treatment of the ill.

14. KINGSTON HIGH SCHOOL
403 Broadway
1913-1915
Arthur Curtis Longyear

Kingston High School was built to replace and consolidate Kingston and Ulster Academies, in Kingston and in Rondout, respectively. Thus the two villages would be joined educationally, as they had been governmentally in the erection of city hall, just across Broadway. The high school looms over Broadway as a grand classical presence inspired by the royal palace of the Louvre in Paris. The long Broadway façade is accented by a central, pedimented pavilion and, at each end, a lesser projecting pavilion lacking a pediment, but with an arch between

5

14. Kingston High School (vintage photo)

columns, much like the composition of the east front of the Louvre. Unlike the Louvre, the high school's windows are extensive and not recessed, so classrooms would be flooded with light and open to fresh air. Together with the nearby city library and post office, the high school stood for the renewed spirit of classicism in early-twentieth-century America that would not only elevate public taste, but also encourage higher civic virtues among the people. (In 1919 the trio of classical buildings was joined briefly by a classical Victory Arch over Broadway, designed by Gerard Betz.)

The architect, Arthur Curtis Longyear was selected through a competition involving eleven entrants, including Alfred Hopkins and Charles S. Keefe (of New York and Kingston), and Myron Teller and Beverly King (of the same cities). Longyear had already designed several schools, including the Brigham School (1899-1901) on O'Neil Street.

15. KINGSTON CITY LIBRARY
(Kingston City Schools Consolidated)
399 Broadway
1904
Raymond F. Almirall

Organized in 1899 as a result of the efforts of members of the Daughters of the American Revolution, the Kingston City Library occupied space in city hall until March 1904, when the building designed by Raymond F. Almirall opened. Andrew Carnegie provided $30,000. Between 1886 and 1917 Carnegie funds were used in constructing over 1600 libraries. The Carnegie Library of Pittsburgh, West End Branch, which opened in 1899, may have been the source of the Kingston design.

Almirall was a prominent architect in Brooklyn who had studied architecture at Cornell, and then received a diploma from the Ecole des Beaux-Arts in Paris in 1896 when it was considered the world's leading architectural school. The Ecole taught the absolute superiority of classical standards, and Almirall, even without the Pittsburgh precedent, would never have considered following the Gothic style of city hall, across Broadway from the library site. He designed the library façade with ancient Greek classical forms (there are no Roman arches), notably the pedimented pavilion with Ionic columns and acroteria at the corners of the pediment. Slender, so-called "Roman" bricks were fashionable around 1900, and they add to the refinement of the façade and end walls.

Thus, as in other American cities after the triumph of classicism at the Chicago World's Fair of 1893, the civic center, with the library as an important component, was to become mainly classical. Its formal dignity

(like the books of the library) would be an inspiration for good citizenship.
NYS and NR 1995

16. MYRON J. MICHAEL JUNIOR HIGH SCHOOL
(Kingston High School Campus)
55 Andrew Street
1937-1938
Teller and Halverson

By 1930 the French classicism of Kingston High School was falling from favor nationally, in part because of its expense. This junior high school, and especially its Georgian-Federal-style central pavilion with slender pilasters, pediment with oval window, and cupola above, retained the principles of classicism, while being cheaper and more

5

15. Kingston City Library (vintage photo)

16. Myron J. Michael Junior High School (vintage photo)

"American" in appearance than the high school.

In 1935 the Board of Education adopted plans for a junior high school submitted by George E. Lowe in the "English Renaissance or Georgian Colonial" style. These plans were subsequently rejected, and in 1937 a design by Teller and Halverson was selected in an informal competition open to local architects, many of whom were desperate for work during the Depression. The unsuccessful competitors were Augustus A. Schrowang, Albert E. Milliken, and Frederick H. Roosa.

17. J. J. AND FRANK W. ALBRECHT GROCERY
(Arace Electronics)
357-359 Broadway
c. 1896

A faded sign painted on the east wall of 357 Broadway serves as a reminder that this was once the grocery, flour and feed store of Frank W. Albrecht. It is a well-preserved example of the turn-of-the-century commercial building in the Italianate style, with iron columns and sheet metal cornices above the expansive display windows.

17. J. J. and Frank W. Albrecht Grocery

TOUR 6:
INDUSTRIAL DISTRICT
NEAR THE WEST SHORE RAILROAD

n 1902, one promoter of the city as a place for business and industry cited the "scenic environment, nestled here between the great mountains and the broad, deep flowing river," but celebrated also the "massive brick factory walls with chimneys and smoke stacks belching smoke and steam, moving trains, trolley cars, long lines of freight cars, and the low hum of industry floating in the air." With the coming of the West Shore Railroad in 1883, Kingston experienced industrial growth near its tracks, a development ignored or viewed with distaste by "a goodly number of wealthy residents, descendants of the good old Dutch stock" who saw no reason to disturb their comfortable lives. (Howard Hendricks, *The City of Kingston*, 1902)

**Industrial and commercial buildings along the West Shore Railroad
near Broadway in the early twentieth century.**

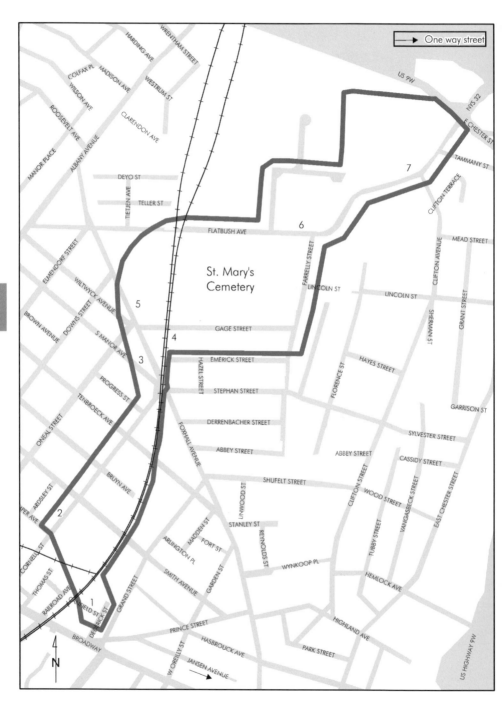

TOUR 6:
INDUSTRIAL DISTRICT
NEAR THE WEST SHORE RAILROAD

1. **G. W. VAN SLYKE AND HORTON**
   (Canfield Supply Co.)
2. **F. JACOBSON & SONS SHIRT FACTORY**
   (formerly)
3. **UNITED STATES LACE CURTAIN MILLS**
   (formerly)
4. **DIAMOND TRUCK AND CAR GEAR COMPANY**
   (formerly)
5. **ST. MARY'S CEMETERY**
6. **COLONIAL GARDENS, KINGSTON HOUSING AUTHORITY**
7. **KINGSTON CITY ALMS HOUSE**
   (Ulster County Health Department)

6

1. G. W. VAN SLYKE AND HORTON
(Canfield Supply Co.)
25 Dederick Street
1907

Van Slyke and Horton, cigar manufacturers, occupied this building that best represents the cigar industry that flourished in turn-of-the-century Kingston. (The former cigar factory of Powell, Smith & Co. on Broadway at Pine Grove Avenue was demolished in 1999.) It also demonstrates that factory buildings of the period were thought worthy of architectural treatment, as seen in the vertical panels of brick and the corner tower with Italianate, paired arched windows and rusticated corners. The name of the factory's designer is unknown; his plans were carried out by contractor John Dyer of Albany.

Within the building were benches for 800 workers in the rolling department alone.

2. F. JACOBSON & SONS SHIRT
FACTORY (formerly)
77 Cornell Street at Smith Avenue
1917 and 1925
Myron S. Teller

Here is further evidence that a factory could be a work of architecture. The Jacobson Shirt Factory was designed with modern steel-sash windows framed by vertical brick panels and slightly recessed spandrels. The stair towers, with rectangular panels in yellow brick, provide distinctive terminal features for the long Cornell Street façade. Originally three stories tall, plans for

1. G. W. Van Slyke and Horton

the fourth story were announced in September 1925.

Understandably, a photo of this factory was featured in "Come to Kingston," a brochure of the 1920s promoting the city as a place to visit, live, and work. The boosterish text identified "modern" factories, like Jacobson's, as "fire proof and incorporating every approved safety device and sanitary and health feature." At Jacobson's, windows composed more than three-quarters of the wall area to provide abundant light and air. Moreover, the brochure proposed that "good feeling and a spirit of cooperation will be found . . . in the manufacturing plants, between employer and employee. Labor disputes are a rarity and strikes practically unknown." Most of Jacobson's workers were young women. The factory was equipped with a dining hall and recreation room on the third floor where lunch time was enlivened by "daily dances and song recitals," and where there were weekly evening "social dances."

But in 2002 Ruth Barringer (born 1913) had less pleasant memories of the Jacobson Factory: "I didn't enjoy ironing shirts. ... We worked on the top floor, no fans. That was a true sweat shop."

The Manhattan Shirt Factory (1919) by Gerard Betz, on Hoffman Street, is a comparable design and was undoubtedly considered another of the city's "modern" factories.

2. F. Jacobson & Sons Shirt Factory

3. UNITED STATES LACE CURTAIN MILLS (formerly)
Foxhall Avenue at Cornell Street
c. 1903

3. United States Lace Curtain Mills

At the beginning of the twentieth century, as the D and H Canal, and the cement and bluestone industries declined in Rondout, the West Shore Railroad and industries along its tracks became important for the city's economic vitality. This textile mill was handsomely designed, with its long walls articulated with vertical brick panels and multi-paned sash windows with stone lintels and sills.

Many of the mill workers were young women. In 1907 a fire threatened their lives, as it did their counterparts in other places with more disastrous results. According to the *Freeman* (November 27, 1907), "some girls who were working on the second floor of the building smelled smoke and soon the smoke made its way up from the floor beneath. There was some excitement and many of the girls were frightened. Cooler counsel prevailed in a short time, however, and some of the men employees were summoned. After a short but fierce fight the flames were extinguished."

6

4. DIAMOND TRUCK AND CAR GEAR COMPANY (formerly)
22-28 Gage Street at West Shore Railroad
c. 1898

Many decades after the closing of the Diamond Truck and Car Gear Company, organized in 1895 as a manufacturer of electric railway car trucks (or wheel assemblies), fragments of its name can still be deciphered, painted in the brick gable facing Gage Street. The factory's long wall adjacent to the railroad tracks is a good example of paneled brickwork with segmental arches characteristic of much well-designed late-nineteenth-century commercial and industrial architecture.

Kingston at the turn of the century was the site of a larger manufacturer of steam and electric railway equipment, the Peckham Manufacturing Co. (later New York Car and Truck Co.) on Hasbrouck Avenue near Grand Street. In December 1899 the *Street Railway Journal* reported that Kingston's Colonial City Traction Co. owned seven closed and six open, or summer, trolley cars mounted on Peckham and Diamond trucks.

5. ST. MARY'S CEMETERY
322 Foxhall Avenue
1869 and later

This Roman Catholic cemetery was organized July 10, 1869, by St. Mary's Church. While laid out on flatter ground less susceptible to picturesque landscape effects than the earlier Protestant cemeteries of Montrepose and Wiltwyck, an 1896 photo (De Lisser, *Picturesque Ulster*, 83) shows the monuments well sheltered by full-grown trees.

Fittingly, the monument of Luke Noone, the Irish-born and trained stone cutter and contractor (see p. 52), is an imposing Celtic cross. James J. Sweeney (died April 5, 1907), owner of a bluestone business (see p. 141), is memorialized by a tall, though conventional, obelisk. The cemetery's most prominent mausoleum, for the McGill family, is a Gothic Revival chapel surmounted by a Celtic cross. Edward T. McGill (1872-1941), whose father had been born in Ireland, was a Kingston dealer in coal, feed, and dairy products, and was very active in St. Mary's Church.

4. Diamond Truck and Car Gear Company

5. St. Mary's Cemetery

6. COLONIAL GARDENS, KINGSTON HOUSING AUTHORITY
Flatbush Avenue
1949-1953
Harry Halverson

State-supported public housing, part of Republican Governor Thomas Dewey's "state-

wide slum clearance and community development program," was a very controversial issue in Kingston in 1949 and 1950. Proponents argued that new, low-cost housing was needed to attract new industries to replace those that had flourished seventy-five years earlier in Rondout, but were now dead or dying. Also, World War II and Korean conflict veterans were entitled to decent, inexpensive housing. Opponents, including the Kingston Taxpayers League, replied that "100 favored families would live cheaply at the expense of other taxpayers," and the project would be a "monument to political corruption." For opponents, subsidized housing essentially amounted to socialism, and was uneconomical; the $11,800 to build a four-room unit was considerably more than the $6,600 cost of a Gunnison Home built by the private sector.

In August 1950 the Kingston Common Council and state officials approved the project, involving 100 units housing about 420

6. Colonial Gardens, Kingston Housing Authority (Halverson drawing)

people in two-story garden apartments. The *Freeman* had noted in 1949 that the State Constitution forbade racial discrimination in the selection of occupants. About twenty percent of the approximately eight-acre site would be built upon; the rest would be landscaped with lawns, walks, and play areas. Abundant sunlight, fresh air, and green grass would compensate for the bland architecture. Halverson's plan, however, did call for a note of formal dignity and civic order in the main axis extending from Flatbush Avenue, through a terrace with flagpole, and terminating in a bold chimney and attached administration building. His plan also had the virtue of banishing cars from the central grassy courts and relegating them to the project's margins.

7. KINGSTON CITY ALMS HOUSE
(Ulster County Health Department)
300 Flatbush Avenue
1872-1874
J. A. Wood

It speaks well of the new city government that the first building it erected was an institution to care (inexpensively) for 150 to 200 of the poor of Kingston. J. A. Wood had already designed the Poughkeepsie City Alms House in 1868, and so he repeated the Italianate elements of that three-part façade in a fashion that alludes to the dignity of municipal government while avoiding expensive ornament. In 1954, the building was remodeled by Harry Halverson to serve as the Ulster County Chronic Infirmary.

7. Kingston City Alms House (vintage photo)

TOUR 7:
CHESTNUT STREET HISTORIC DISTRICT

A century ago the West Chestnut Street hilltop was the site of the mansions of some of Kingston's richest and most powerful families, notably those of Samuel Coykendall (now demolished) and George Smith. Earlier, in the 1850s, landscape painter Jervis McEntee had built his picturesque wooden studio on the same hilltop with views south over the Rondout Creek and north into the Catskills. While his studio is gone, a part of his view can be enjoyed from the circle at the end of West Chestnut Street. McEntee's strolls to visit family graves in Montrepose Cemetery (whose beauty he thought superior to that of the more famous Green-Wood Cemetery in Brooklyn) can be duplicated today, but his longer hikes that took him over the West Shore Railroad bridge crossing the Rondout are not safely repeated today.

Pennington photo of Mrs. Schoonmaker's garden on West Chestnut Street, 1919.

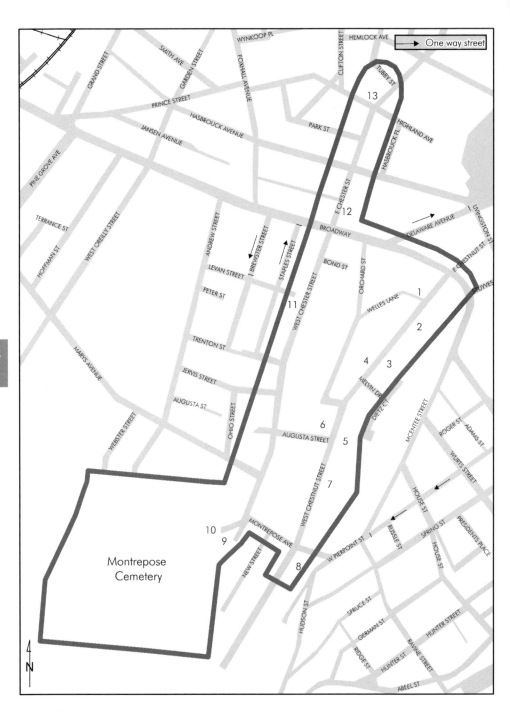

One way street

Montrepose Cemetery

TOUR 7:
CHESTNUT STREET HISTORIC DISTRICT

1. JOHN GILL HOUSE
2. HENRY A. SAMSON HOUSE
3. "CLOVERLY," JAMES L. VAN DEUSEN HOUSE
4. GEORGE COYKENDALL HOUSE
5. GEORGE J. SMITH HOUSE
6. COYKENDALL COACH HOUSE
   (Coach House Players)
7. EDWARD COYKENDALL HOUSE
8. ULSTER ACADEMY AND SCHOOL NO. 2
   (formerly)
9. FRANCES M. REED HOUSE
10. MONTREPOSE CEMETERY
11. HOYSRADT HOUSE
12. KINGSTON CITY ELECTRIC RAILWAY CO. CAR BARN
    (Kingston City Schools Consolidated)
13. INDUSTRIAL HOME OF KINGSTON FOR ORPHAN CHILDREN
    (Good Shepherd School, Morningstar Christian
    Fellowship)

7

1. JOHN GILL HOUSE
19 West Chestnut Street
1870
John Gill?

The *Kingston Journal* reported August 3, 1870, that the builder John Gill had nearly completed a fine new building of brick and cut stone on Chestnut Street. Gill himself occupied the Italianate house, one of Kingston's best-composed and best-preserved examples of the style. Its Italianate features include the low-pitched roofs, bracketed eaves, stone quoins and quoin-like treatment of the circular and round-arched window frames. Picturesque elements are the L-plan, bay windows, and veranda with wooden scrollwork.

In 1872 Gill erected a "handsome new French-roofed, cement concrete house" on the adjoining lot, 15 West Chestnut. This house is pictured in the 1875 Beers *Atlas* as the residence of Hiram Roosa, an insurance and real estate man. The Roosa house's façade resembles Gill's, but was distinguished by its

mansard roof and concrete walls, a product of the local cement industry.
NYS and NR 1985

2. HENRY A. SAMSON HOUSE
32 West Chestnut Street
c. 1853

2. Henry A. Samson House

One of the earliest grandly-designed buildings in Rondout, the Samson house is an orderly, cubical house constructed of dressed bluestone. Its style is Italianate, evident in the broad eaves supported by paired brackets and in the round-arched second-story windows. The arches are composed of two marble segments on each side of a keystone. Also Italianate are the low-pitched roof, central cupola (enhancing the view of the Hudson River and Rondout Creek), and even the recessed arches of the chimneys.

Samson (1818-1869) gained wealth as a tanner in the Catskills, then as a banker and associate of Thomas Cornell. His architect may have been Calvert Vaux, whose Marine Villa in Newport, Rhode Island, has similar Italianate details and whose father-in-law, James McEntee, was a previous owner of the site.
NYS and NR 1985

1. John Gill House

3. "Cloverly," James L. Van Deusen House

3. "CLOVERLY," JAMES L. VAN DEUSEN HOUSE
70 West Chestnut Street
1891

This splendid example of the late-nine-teenth-century Colonial Revival was the residence of James L. Van Deusen, partner in a wholesale drug business. It was probably conceived by an architect (as yet unidentified) who was accustomed to designing in the medieval revivals using picturesque compositions. Bits of the eighteenth-century American Georgian and Federal styles—Palladian and oval windows, white columned porches, gambrel roofs—are distributed with none of the order or sense of proportion of those styles. And what could have been the colonial precedent for the polygonal tower overlooking the Rondout? Colonial Revival architects of the next generation, such as Myron Teller and Charles Keefe, would have thought their own work infinitely more correct and in good taste. NYS and NR 1985

4. GEORGE COYKENDALL HOUSE
77 West Chestnut Street
c. 1896
Addison E. Dederick, general contactor and builder

George Coykendall, engaged in the management of the Stony Clove Railroad and Kingston City Railroad, was a brother of Kingston's most prominent businessman of the period, Samuel D. Coykendall, whose hulking, turreted mansion designed by Calvert Vaux once stood at 90 West Chestnut Street. George's lesser success is told in his residence's more modest scale. Still, it is an accomplished design, a nicely unified picturesque composition. This is especially true of the street façade, which ties together walls of brick and brown sandstone below with patterned wood shingles above, as well as a classical porch and window details (including an Adamesque garland) with a medieval, Richardsonian cylindrical turret and conical roof.
NYS and NR 1985

4. George Coykendall House

5. George J. Smith House

5. GEORGE J. SMITH HOUSE
124 West Chestnut Street
c. 1893
Arthur Curtis Longyear

Samuel D. Coykendall (1837-1913) and cigar manufacturer George J. Smith (1859-1913) were powerful forces in Kingston business and politics. Smith, through Powell, Smith and Co., employed some 1100 workers in Kingston and 500 in New York City. Their large Kingston factory, completed in 1891

and located on Broadway at Pine Grove Avenue, was demolished in 1999. Smith was a leading Republican and served in Congress, 1903-1905. His power, like Coykendall's, was expressed in the bulky grandeur of his house. Both houses were sited atop the West Chestnut Street hill, and both were pictured under construction on the same page of *Art Work of Ulster County* in 1893.

For Smith, New York architect Arthur Curtis Longyear designed a picturesquely towered and turreted fortress with heavily rusticated stonework on the first story. The second story was lighter, of brick, and the original porches and balustrades, as well as the upper story of the round tower, were given light, classical details. In addition to the towers, there was a balustraded lookout atop the main roof, which would have provided extensive views of the Rondout and Hudson. In the later twentieth century the house fell into disrepair, but a restoration has been underway in recent years.

6. COYKENDALL COACH HOUSE
(Coach House Players)
12 Augusta Street
c. 1894

With its many gables, cupolas, dormers, diamond-paned casements, and sections of half-timbering, this coach house was Old World picturesque and a suitable adjunct to the fortress-like (but no longer extant) main house of Samuel Coykendall. The coach house gave the property some of the distinction the F. W. Vanderbilts achieved with the

6. Coykendall Coach House

help of their larger but similarly styled coach or carriage house in Hyde Park. In 1950, Albert E. Milliken prepared plans for converting this building into a theater seating 250.

7. EDWARD COYKENDALL HOUSE
166 West Chestnut Street
c. 1912
York and Sawyer

A fine example of the urban mansion in classical style, Edward Coykendall's house represented a reaction against the picturesque, medieval revival mansion designed by Calvert Vaux for Edward's father, Samuel Coykendall, at 90 West Chestnut Street. Edward's house was designed by the prominent New York architectural firm of York and Sawyer, who also designed the classical Coykendall Memorial at Montrepose Cemetery. Resembling an American Georgian house in its low hipped roof and balustrade above the eaves, Edward's residence was given a Continental air by being expanded to seven bays with stuccoed walls and tall French windows, and enriched with a pedimented Doric doorway in marble. Originally the house had one-story wings to the east and west, as well as finely landscaped grounds. The pergola at the rear of the house resembled the pergola of the Coykendall Memorial. After the death of Isabel Hutton Coykendall in 1928, her husband Edward published a handsomely bound memorial book of photographs of the garden.

Edward Coykendall (1871-1949) was a graduate of Columbia University in engineering and carried on his father's business interests, especially as president of the Ulster and Delaware Railroad. His concern for civic improvement, including beautification, led him to be active on the boards of Kingston Hospital, Montrepose Cemetery, and the Senate House.

7. Edward Coykendall House

8. ULSTER ACADEMY AND SCHOOL NO. 2 (formerly)
214 West Chestnut Street
1870, 1886
R. G. Blum, Charles W. Romeyn

In 1896 this was the county's largest school, with students from the primary grades through college preparatory courses. Like other Kingston schools of the 1870s, to please taxpayers, the school's exterior originally was plain, with modest cornice and segmental-

8. Ulster Academy and School No. 2 (vintage photo)

arched windows. Additions made in 1886, designed by Charles W. Romeyn, included the Chestnut Street façade with brick pilasters over the second and third stories, and a handsome, pyramidal-roofed tower with swelling, battered wall at its base and triple-arched upper story. Romeyn had designed a similar tower about 1884 for the New Paltz Academy (destroyed by fire, 1906).

Romeyn, a New York architect trained in Calvert Vaux's office and with family roots in Kingston, was employed because he was recommended by the artist Jervis McEntee to Academy trustee William Winter and Samuel Coykendall. McEntee felt that Blum's 1870 building was full of "awful monstrosities," and that Romeyn's talents had been proven by his redesign of the Kingston Academy, which stood on Academy Green until 1916. (McEntee Diary, June 19 and July 2, 1886)

Because the building was sited on a plateau high above the Rondout, the school's upper windows furnished "views ... of the country that is grand and far-reaching," including the Hudson, Berkshires, Catskills, and Shawangunks. The high elevation also had the beneficial effect of providing "air, wafted from the Catskills ... pure and invigorating."

9. FRANCES M. REED HOUSE
75 Montrepose Avenue
1906
Thomas P. Rice?

The superintendent's residence of Montrepose Cemetery since 1927, this was originally the private home of Frances M. Reed (1840-1924), grieving widow of Alonzo Reed (1841-1899). Women were rarely architectural clients in 1906, and even in this case Mrs. Reed was acting out of devotion to her late husband. Alonzo Reed had been

buried near the cemetery gate, and his widow "purchased the plot of ground just outside the main cemetery entrance and had the house erected for her home where she could overlook the grave of her husband during her lifetime." (*Freeman,* December 31, 1926)

Built of bluestone, including a sill inscribed 1906, the Reed house resembles the larger James J. Sweeney house (c. 1896) at 67 Wurts Street. The main block of both houses is symmetrical, with a hipped roof and low turret above the classically-detailed porch. Perhaps because it was to be occupied by a single woman, the Reed house rises only a story and a half, incorporating seven rooms and a bath.

In *Kingston, N.Y., Illustrated and Descriptive* (1906), Thomas P. Rice described himself as an "architect" with twelve years experience as "carpenter and builder." He also took credit for the construction of the Reed house, and he may have designed it.

9. Frances M. Reed House

10. MONTREPOSE CEMETERY
75 Montrepose Avenue
1849 and later

After being organized in 1849 as the Cemetery Association of Rondout, and reorganized the next year as Montrepose

10. Montrepose Cemetery

Cemetery, twenty acres were purchased in May 1850 and lots surveyed by C. S. Quilliard, who became the cemetery's superintendent. In 1911 Quilliard was described as "an engineer brought up in Paris." Like Wiltwyck Rural Cemetery, Montrepose was designed as a romantic park with roadways placed in relation to the rolling contours of the land. The natural landscape was cultivated to enhance Christian sentiments about mortality and the afterlife. Quilliard's 1850 map of the cemetery indicated the site of a chapel, which probably was never built; since 1897 the site has been occupied by the columnar monument of the Rondout Masons. The map also included a marginal vignette of a hilly landscape with evergreen tree and the legend, "through night to light."

Among the notable nineteenth-century monuments are those of Jervis McEntee, the Hudson River School painter, his wife, Anna

Gertrude McEntee, and his brother-in-law, the celebrated architect, Calvert Vaux. Anna Gertrude McEntee's monument, adorned with finely carved morning glories, was designed in 1880 by her husband, Jervis, and her nephew, Downing Vaux. As we know from Jervis's diary, morning glories were his favorite flowers (roses were hers), and he placed them about her in her coffin, and on the coffin.

Early-twentieth-century classical designs include a 1909 monument to Thomas Chambers, Kingston's founder, unveiled on the city's 250th anniversary. Charles Rollinson Lamb (1860-1942), designer of the monument, was a New York architect and specialist in memorials. He was probably chosen by Judge A. T. Clearwater, chairman of the anniversary celebration's executive committee. The memorial gardens of the Coykendall family, by York and Sawyer (photos were published in the *Architectural Record*, May 1917), dominate a rise in the cemetery just as the mansions of Samuel and Edward Coykendall dominated West Chestnut Street. The Louise Schoonmaker Chilton memorial (c. 1930) was designed by landscape architect Prentiss French and sculptor Margaret French Cresson (her father was the noted sculptor Daniel Chester French).

11. HOYSRADT HOUSE
53 West Chester Street
c. 1895

This Queen Anne-style house with multiple gables and projecting bays, decoratively patterned shingles, and a frieze of spindles ornamenting the porch, was built for Louis Hoysradt. His daughter, Emily Hoysradt, a Kingston artist who painted murals in the Governor Clinton Hotel, resided here and maintained her studio in the attic until her death in 1983.

11. Hoysradt House

12. KINGSTON CITY ELECTRIC RAILWAY CO. CAR BARN (Kingston City Schools Consolidated)
East Chester Street at Broadway
c. 1897

12. Kingston City Electric Railway Co. Car Barn

Although much altered, this is the principal surviving artifact of the street railways that served Kingstonians, first with horse cars in 1866, and then with electric trolleys until 1930 when the last trolley car gave way to buses. The 1892 Sanborn Map indicates a brick building on this site, identified as "Kingston City Street R. R. Stables." Its long façade faced East Chester Street. In 1897, the Kingston City Railroad, electrified in 1893, constructed a seventy-foot extension, probably the section of the present building having Italianate brackets and segmental-arched windows that runs parallel to Broadway. A 1901 blueprint for new track work made by Pennsylvania Steel Company, Steelton, Pennsylvania, shows a single track entering the car barn through the broad door on East Chester Street. Within the building, that track divided into nine tracks running parallel to Broadway. Short segments of the original trolley tracks remain within the building, and a piece of rail serves as the lintel for the office door on East Chester Street.

Samuel D. Coykendall was president of the Kingston City Railroad in the 1890s. A rival company, the Colonial City Electric Railroad, had its car barn (c. 1893), smaller and plainer than Kingston City's, on Smith Avenue at the West Shore Railroad crossing. It, too, survives, but neither building reveals its original function. In 1901, the two companies were joined as the Kingston Consolidated Railroad Co., and by 1907 all trolleys operated from the East Chester Street barn.

13. INDUSTRIAL HOME OF KINGSTON FOR ORPHAN CHILDREN
(Good Shepherd School, Morningstar Christian Fellowship)
77 East Chester Street
1903

Organized in 1876, the Industrial Home was open to homeless children of all creeds and races. In 1881, J. A. Wood donated a plan for a permanent home for the institution, but not until 1903 was such a home erected;

the architect of the 1903 building is as yet unidentified. Mary Isabella Forsyth (1841-1914), founder and president of the Trustees and Managers of the Home, wrote of its aim to save the city and county "money, health, and morals. Pauperism gives way, disease is overcome, character is uplifted, whole families are influenced for the good." (Industrial Home, *Report*, 1909)

Architecturally, the Home resembles settlement houses of the period in its domestic and relatively non-institutional exterior. The deep porch and many windows imply a concern for fresh air, conducive to good health. The simple paneling of the brick walls, and picturesque dormers in the steep, hipped roof, suggest both frugality and a desire to provide a home of unpretentious good taste, perhaps influencing character for the better.

The cornerstone was laid in 1903 by Governor Benjamin B. Odell, Jr., at the celebration of the 250th anniversary of the settlement of Esopus, later Kingston. It is inscribed with notable events in Kingston's colonial history, surely at the suggestion of Mary Isabella Forsyth.

7

13. Industrial Home of Kingston for Orphan Children

Rondout waterfront in the late nineteenth century.

TOUR 8:
RONDOUT HISTORIC DISTRICT

Rondout was a busy center of canal and river commerce after the opening of the Delaware and Hudson Canal in 1828. In the mid-nineteenth century it also had the reputation of being a rough and rowdy place, but by the early 1870s many churches and schools had been put up, which gave the district an aura of respectability. In 1880, Nathaniel Bartlett Sylvester found several of Rondout's churches were graced with "splendid architecture," and the adjacent late-nineteenth-century photograph represents the towers of two churches punctuating the skyline above Rondout Creek. The creek is lined with canal boats, a train on the tracks of the Ulster and Delaware Railroad, and commercial buildings, including the Delaware and Hudson office building at the center of the photo and just to the right of the Greek Revival tower of the Rondout Presbyterian Church.

Sylvester also noted that "pleasant residences"—presumably those of Thomas Cornell on Wurts Street and others on West Chestnut Street—were "located above the dust, noise and confusion of the lower business streets." The artist Jervis McEntee (1828-1891), who maintained a home and studio in Rondout, but also moved in sophisticated New York art circles, walked one day in 1883 from his hilltop home in Rondout down to its commercial center. He observed: "The place had quite a city air with the new Cornell building approaching completion. The streets were all dug up laying the water pipes and there was an air of business and prosperity." (McEntee diary, October 23, 1883)

8

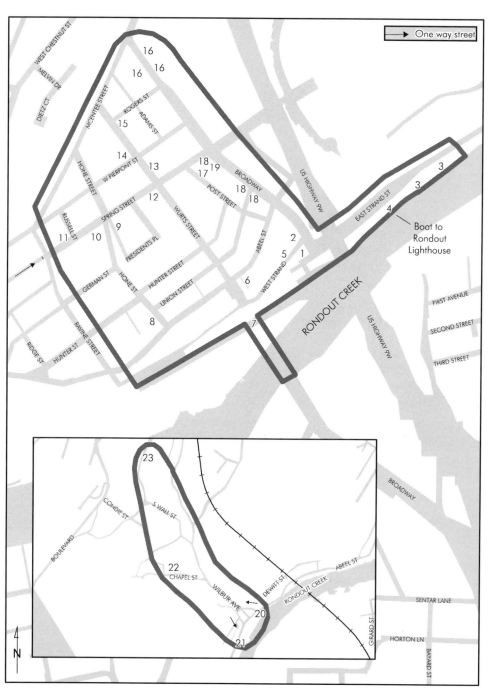

TOUR 8:
RONDOUT HISTORIC DISTRICT

1. **SAMPSON-FREEMAN BUILDING**
2. **MANSION HOUSE**
3. **CORNELL STEAMBOAT COMPANY BOILER SHOP
   AND REPAIR SHOP**
4. **RONDOUT LIGHTHOUSE**
   (Hudson River Maritime Museum)
5. **WEST STRAND COMMERCIAL BUILDINGS**
6. **TEMPLE EMANUEL**
   (West Strand Grill)
7. **RONDOUT CREEK BRIDGE**
   (Kingston-Port Ewen Suspension Bridge)
8. **THOMAS BURGESS HOUSE**
9. **TRINITY GERMAN EVANGELICAL LUTHERAN CHURCH**
10. **TUBBY ROW**
11. **CONRAD HILTEBRANT HOUSE**
12. **JAMES J. SWEENEY HOUSE**
13. **EPISCOPAL CHURCH OF THE HOLY SPIRIT**
    (St. Mark's African Methodist Episcopal Church)
14. **ST. PETER'S ROMAN CATHOLIC CHURCH**
15. **ENGLISH EVANGELICAL LUTHERAN CHURCH OF THE REDEEMER**
    (Redeemer Lutheran Church)
16. **ST. MARY'S ROMAN CATHOLIC CHURCH, SCHOOL, RECTORY
    AND CONVENT**
17. **THOMAS CORNELL CARRIAGE HOUSE**
18. **COMMERCIAL BUILDINGS**
19. **JEWISH COMMUNITY CENTER**
    (Kingston Community Development)
20. **SIMEON AND WILLIAM B. FITCH OFFICE**
21. **THOMAS J. FEENEY ENTERPRISES**
22. **SWEENEY HOUSE-FATHER DIVINE PEACE MISSION**
23. **MOUNT ZION CEMETERY**

8

1. SAMPSON-FREEMAN BUILDING
1 Broadway at West Strand
1875
Henry Engelbert

The Sampson Building, including the Sampson & Ellis clothing and shoe store with an opera house above, was, when new, described as the "most ornate and impressive" business building in Rondout. (*Daily Freeman*, March 12, 1875) This assertion was certainly inspired by the mansard roof and tower, which were destroyed by fire in 1885. Still, Engelbert's design remains noteworthy, thanks in large part to the ground story's thirty-one cast-iron columns and piers that originally framed plate-glass display windows. The pier bases identify the maker: McEntee and Dillon Rondout Ironworks. In the twentieth century the building was occupied by the *Freeman*.

Henry Engelbert, a New York architect, was also responsible for the German Lutheran church on Spring Street (1873-1875). In New York, his Bond Street Savings Bank (1874) was clad in cast iron and had a mansard roof. NYS and NR 1979

2. MANSION HOUSE
Broadway at West Strand
1854

The Mansion House was Rondout's principal hotel during the village's heyday in the third quarter of the nineteenth century. Strategically located near the landing for New York and Albany steamboats, it also had stages leaving from its door for Kingston, Delhi, and Ellenville in the 1850s.

The present building was erected, according to local historian Kathleen Burton,

1. Sampson-Freeman Building

8

2. Mansion House (lithograph by William W. Rose, 1885, collection of The New-York Historical Society)

on the site of an earlier hotel of the same name, which was opened in 1832 by James S. McEntee, engineer for the Delaware and Hudson Canal Company. Today's Mansion House was built in 1854 for Major George Francis Von Beck (1798-1870) and accommodated tourists and commercial travelers in its one hundred "sleeping compartments," while a post office and shops were located in the ground story.

The simply designed brick walls with stone lintels and sills were enlivened by paired Italianate brackets at the eaves, and, more strikingly, by the cast-iron grills of the balconies and imposing staircase leading to the main entrance at the Broadway-West Strand corner. In 1886 this stone staircase, called "ugly" by the *Freeman*, was replaced by plate glass windows. Above the same corner, a domed cupola with clock and scrollwork at its base once served as a lookout and beacon attracting patrons.

NYS and NR 1979

3. CORNELL STEAMBOAT COMPANY BOILER SHOP AND REPAIR SHOP
East Strand
c. 1892 and 1901

3. Cornell Steamboat Company Boiler Shop

Along with the former Fitch Office on Abeel Street, these two shop buildings are the main architectural reminders of the river commerce that helped Kingston flourish in the late nineteenth century. The shops serviced the tugs of the Cornell Steamboat Co. and so are directly on Rondout Creek. An architectural drawing of the boiler shop (c. 1892) is signed "T. C. C." Thomas Cornell Coykendall (1866-1934), son of Samuel Coykendall, was a Columbia University-trained engineer in charge of the Cornell shops. Its great arched windows and central raised monitor roof enhanced light and air, but also gave it something of the appearance of an industrial sanctuary. The decorative woodwork above the central doorway furthers the idea that making and repairing boilers was compatible with the art of architecture. Oval iron panels bolted to the brick corner piers resemble those of Andrew Mason's 1888 section of District School No. 8, now the Kingston Library on Franklin Street. In 1950, as diesel engines replaced

steam, the boiler shop was sold to B. Millens and Sons for steel fabrication.

The imposing brick mass of the repair shop is less visible today than is the boiler shop. A glimpse of the vast interior space can be obtained by looking into the upper-level windows from across the East Strand. Architectural drawings reveal that the repair shop was designed in the company's offices; the drawings are dated August 8 and 10, 1901, and were approved by Ivor Jungquist, chief draftsman and engineer.
NYS and NR 1980

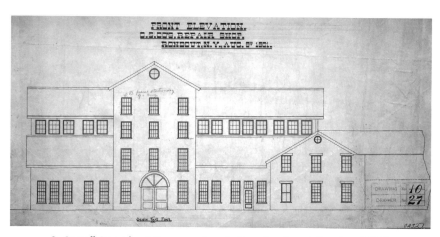

3. Cornell Steamboat Company Repair Shop (unsigned drawing, 1901)

4. Rondout Lighthouse

4. RONDOUT LIGHTHOUSE (Hudson River Maritime Museum)
Hudson River at the mouth of Rondout Creek
1913-1915
Office of the Lighthouse Inspector, Third District (Tompkinsville, N.Y.)

The romance of lighthouses—isolated beacons warning mariners of dangerous waters, as well as dwellings for their keepers—and the customary beauty of their locations combine to separate them from mundane architectural commentary. Still, Hudson River lighthouses were affected by the same stylistic changes that are found in ordinary houses. The mansard roofs of the Esopus Meadows and Hudson-Athens lighthouses mark them as designs of the 1870s. The present Rondout Lighthouse (it was preceded by others built in 1837 and 1867) shows, in the treatment of the gables as pediments and in the use of corner pilasters, the federal government's preference for classical forms in the early twentieth

century. The walls and piers, however, look remarkably solid and plain—strong enough to hold back storms—in contrast to the nearly contemporary and more decorative post office (see p. 175). Blueprints dated 1914 indicate that the floors were built using the "Kahn system of Reinforced Concrete."

The light of this structure was first lit August 15, 1915. Automation in 1954 and the departure of the keeper led to structural deterioration over the next decades. Since 1984 the Hudson River Maritime Museum has leased the structure and, with the City of Kingston, is working towards a restoration of exterior and interior. The Coast Guard continues to maintain the white light which flashes every six seconds.
NYS and NR 1979; open to public

5. WEST STRAND COMMERCIAL BUILDINGS
9-29 West Strand
c. 1870

8

5. West Strand Commercial Buildings

These waterfront commercial buildings once served the everyday needs of Rondout residents and those connected with its busy port. Here, and nearby on Broadway, are the remnants of a vital late-nineteenth-century business district, much of which fell to urban renewal in the 1960s. These seven survivors were harmoniously, but not uniformly, designed, most having Italianate bracketed cornices and arched windows. Four have cast-iron lintels. The ground floor storefronts usually have large display windows and cast-iron piers. Molded into the bases of the simplified classical piers is the name of the local foundry, Rondout Iron Works, whose proprietors in 1871 were John McEntee and John Dillon. The same foundry also may have been responsible for the iron lintels and railings seen throughout Rondout. Iron acanthus leaf capitals remain at 13 and 15 West Strand, which in 1922 was the shop of

R. W. Anderson & Co., who did fine printing. Acanthus leaf capitals were susceptible to rust, hence their low survival rate.
NYS and NR 1974; HLPC

6. TEMPLE EMANUEL
(West Strand Grill)
50 Abeel Street
1891-1892
Adolph Fleischmann

Temple Emanuel's street façade clearly expressed that here was a place of Jewish worship. While the round arches derive from the medieval Romanesque (like St. Peter's Roman Catholic Church on Wurts Street), Jewish tradition was proclaimed in two tablets of the Law embedded in the brick wall, three metal Stars of David that once appeared on the roofline, and another Star

6. Temple Emanuel (photo 1976)

of David in the large, circular, stained glass window. (This window is now visible at the Albany Avenue synagogue to which the con-gregation moved in 1958.) The corner towers were topped with "minarets ... in imitation of the Moorish style." The larger of the two, on

137

the eastern corner, has been removed, but had eight columns with carved capitals and was a scaled-down version of the towers of New York's Temple Emanu-El (1866-1868). Dr. Gustav Gottheil of the New York temple dedicated the Rondout temple on September 14, 1892. The architect, Adolph Fleischmann, had, with Isaac Perry, designed Albany's Temple Beth Emeth (1887-1889) with massive Richardsonian Romanesque stonework.

Rondout's Congregation Emanuel was incorporated in 1854 by German Jews, most of whom had come to America in 1848. In the 1890s it became a Reform congregation. NYS and NR 1979; HLPC

7. Rondout Creek Bridge

7. RONDOUT CREEK BRIDGE
(Kingston-Port Ewen Suspension Bridge)
Foot of Wurts Street
1919-1921
Daniel Moran, Engineer; Terry-Tench Co., General Contractors

The Rondout Creek Bridge, a graceful suspension bridge joining Rondout and Port Ewen, was a modest triumph of early-twentieth-century engineering and a clear sign of the coming of the automobile age to Kingston when it opened for traffic in 1922 and replaced the chain ferry "Skillypot." The bridge was a state project; the bill calling for construction of the bridge was signed a decade before its completion. Various plans made between 1914 and 1919 called for a bridge of massive concrete and steel construction with piers extending down to rock below the creek bed. Completion was delayed by World War I, local political strife, and the discovery that the creek bed did not permit building piers in midstream. Therefore, a suspension bridge was required.

Colonel F. S. Greene, State Commissioner of Highways, announced the selection of Daniel Moran's design for the steel suspension bridge in September 1919. (Moran later was one of the designers of the Mid-Hudson suspension bridge at Poughkeepsie, and he was a consultant on the George Washington Bridge.) The roadway and sidewalks are suspended above the creek from two great cables, each cable composed of 1,974 wires, and each wire capable of supporting three tons. The steel towers and trusses of the Rondout bridge resemble those of the privately-built Bear Mountain Bridge (1923-1924), although the Bear Mountain Bridge is longer and higher.

The cornerstone of Ulster County bluestone, visible on the Kingston approach to the bridge, was laid by Governor Alfred E. Smith on September 18, 1920. It was furnished by the Hudson River Bluestone Co. Bluestone, however, was a declining industry

8

in 1920 when steel (in this case made in Pittsburgh) was in the ascendancy. One of the welders of the steel fabric was Mrs. Catherine Nelson, said to be "the only woman welder in the world." The *Freeman* reported (September 6, 1921) that she was to be the subject of a Pathé news reel.

The Rondout Creek is also crossed further upstream at Wilbur, by the West Shore Railroad, which in 1904 replaced its original bridge with a stronger steel–truss bridge. Two workers, Joseph Weber and Richard E. Conklin, were killed in falls while constructing this bridge.

NYS and NR 1980

8. THOMAS BURGESS HOUSE
15 Hone Street
1837

This Federal-style house stands on a lot purchased by Thomas Burgess from the Delaware and Hudson Canal Co. for $150 in 1833. The 1858 Rondout *Directory* refers to Burgess's business as "sectional docks." The front portion of the house is believed to date 1837, because a mortgage was taken out that year for $1100.

The brick Hone Street façade is a good example of the Federal-style urban house with refined classical details, particularly the doorway flanked by Ionic columns and topped with an elliptical-arched fanlight. Façade lintels and sills, and the water table atop the basement wall, are of red sandstone, unusual in Kingston and probably imported from Connecticut. Burgess's funds apparently did not permit brick and stone to be used beyond the façade—the side walls are of wide boards. In the late nineteenth century a bracketed porch was built across the façade; this was removed in a thorough restoration of the front by the Friends of Historic Kingston in 1981. In 1977-1978 the Friends had restored

the similar (but more Grecian) Macauley-DeWitt House (c. 1836) at 20 John Street.

NYS and NR 1979; HLPC

8. Thomas Burgess House

9. TRINITY GERMAN EVANGELICAL LUTHERAN CHURCH
72 Spring Street at Hone Street
1873-1875
Henry Engelbert

In the 1870s, Trinity Lutheran's services were conducted in German, and the German name of the congregation is inscribed in a panel on the façade: "Deutsche Ev. Luth. Dreifaltigkeits Kirche." Henry Engelbert's design is Germanic medieval round-arched (including the corbel table of the façade), but with Gothic spire, pinnacles, and wall buttresses. Fine cast-iron gateposts mark the entry to the churchyard. Tall cast-iron columns support the interior nave and aisle vaulting.

Engelbert was a successful New York architect with commissions for a number of Roman Catholic churches, among them the altering of old Saint Patrick's (1868) and a new building for Holy Cross Church (1870). The latter, on West 42nd Street, is especially comparable to his Rondout church.
NYS and NR 1979; HLPC

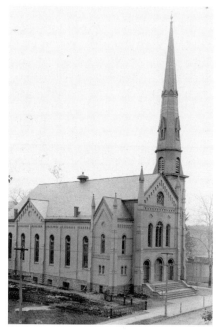

9. Trinity German Evangelical Lutheran Church (vintage photo)

10. TUBBY ROW
Spring Street at Hone Street
1870

Tubby Row was named for its builders, the painter Joseph Tubby and his building contractor father. While not large, the houses were made distinctive with the continuous mansard roof, which allowed the attics to be more spacious, and decorated cast-iron lintels. Tall French windows open upon the long porch, which was a later addition. An early

photograph shows that the doorway of each house was fitted with an individual stoop. The interiors were advertised as having, according to Bob Steuding (*Rondout: A Hudson River Port*), "white marble fireplaces, pale parquet floors, and a view of Rondout Creek." The view began, however, with a brewery just below the houses. In 1880, the brewery belonged to Valentine Thiele. Steuding reports that the Tubbys' building venture was a financial failure.

Joseph Tubby (1821-1896) was originally a house and sign painter. He became a self-taught landscape painter, completing many views of Kingston and vicinity, and sometimes accompanying his friend, Jervis McEntee, on walking tours of the Catskills and Adirondacks.
NYS and NR 1979; HLPC

10. Tubby Row (vintage photo)

11. CONRAD HILTEBRANT HOUSE
101 Spring Street
c. 1890
Albert Mauterstock

Conrad Hiltebrant was a ship builder in South Rondout. In 1892 he advertised his "steam floating drydock with patent adjustable keel block. Lifting capacity about 600 tons." By

11. Conrad Hiltebrant House

1896 he was said to have the largest boat yard on the Rondout Creek.

His residence followed the current vogue for the Queen Anne style, here in wood, with its multiple gables, patterned shingles curving over the first and second stories, and sunburst motifs in the gable peaks. Like the Dr. Elbert Loughran house (1883) at 25 Main Street, there is a beveled corner with window, but overall the refinements of New York architect E. A. Sargent are absent here. Mauterstock, a Rondout native, was trained as a carpenter, and by 1896 called himself a "contractor, manufacturer and builder ... making a specialty of manufacturing moldings, inside fancy woodwork, etc." But he also adopted the title "architect" in describing his role in creating the County Home (1888) in New Paltz and the Hiltebrant house.

12. JAMES J. SWEENEY HOUSE
67 Wurts Street
c. 1896

James J. Sweeney was the son of James Sweeney, founder of a bluestone business continued by his widow, James J., and his brother William. In the 1890s the firm's annual output was 50,000 to 70,000 tons of bluestone, primarily from a thousand acres of quarry land in the towns of Kingston, Hurley, Woodstock, and Ulster. Sweeney stone had been used in building the Washington Monument and the State, War and Navy Building in Washington, and also the Tiffany mansion by McKim, Mead & White in New York.

This Sweeney house, therefore, was constructed of bluestone and, thanks to its prominent location, would have publicized

8

the family business much as the Fitch office building did. There is even a central turret here comparable to the Fitch's. The Sweeney house, however, lacks the exuberant detail of the 1870s, adhering instead to the more disciplined and restrained taste of the 1890s. The hipped roof, simple wooden porch columns, and delicate balusters originally above the porch and defining the widow's walk—these all belonged to the Colonial Revival.
NYS and NR 1979; HLPC

12. James J. Sweeney House

13. EPISCOPAL CHURCH OF THE HOLY SPIRIT (St. Mark's African Methodist Episcopal Church)
72 Wurts Street
1861

This was built as an Episcopal church in the Early English Gothic style with narrow, pointed-arched windows or lancets, wall buttresses, and a bell tower placed picturesquely off the central axis. The design resembles Gothic Revival churches by New York architect Richard Upjohn (1802-1878), the leading designer of Episcopal churches in the mid-nineteenth-century, who believed that the Gothic was uniquely suitable for the High Church rituals which he espoused. The poly-

chrome roof indicates the influence of the Italian Gothic and the taste of the English critic, John Ruskin.

In 1924 the church vestry decided to dissolve the congregation and close the church because of declining membership. Upjohn would undoubtedly have been surprised to learn that between 1926 and 1966 the building served as the place of worship for Congregation Ahavath Israel. In 1927 the cross that had crowned the building and marked it as Christian was moved to Montrepose Cemetery, where it stands as the monument over the grave of William Boyd (1851-1927), erected by his sister, Mrs. Eliza Boyd Purvis (1859-1935).
NYS and NR 1979; HLPC

13. Episcopal Church of the Holy Spirit

14. ST. PETER'S ROMAN CATHOLIC CHURCH
91 Wurts Street
1871-1873
Henry Engelbert

**14. St. Peter's Roman Catholic Church
(photo 1958)**

St. Peter's was organized in 1850 as a parish for German-speaking Catholics. The Irish parish, St. Mary's, had been formed fifteen years earlier. Perhaps to set themselves apart architecturally from the Irish, Rondout's German Catholics employed a German-American architect practicing in New York City, Henry Engelbert, according to information provided by Kathleen Burton. The *Rondout Freeman* (August 18, 1871) reported that the brick building would be in the "Gothic style," but it is actually Romanesque in the round-arched, German medieval style, which was often revived in mid-nineteenth-century Germany. Very characteristic of the Romanesque style are the small arches of the corbel tables that run beneath the cornices and the triple openings of the tower. A spire

once rose from the tower. Engelbert also designed Trinity Evangelical Lutheran Church nearby on Spring Street, for German Protestants.
NYS and NR 1979; HLPC

15. ENGLISH EVANGELICAL LUTHERAN CHURCH OF THE REDEEMER (Redeemer Lutheran Church)
104 Wurts Street
1911-1913
Bannister & Schell

The Gothic Revival appeared in many guises. This English Lutheran church reflects its separation in 1896-1897 from Trinity

15. English Evangelical Lutheran Church of the Redeemer (vintage photo)

German Lutheran on Spring Street, and from the Victorian era, by its low proportions, light-colored stone (St. Lawrence marble with Indiana limestone trim), and more consistently Gothic details. Among Kingston's Gothic Revival churches, it is the closest to the designs of the leading Gothic Revivalists of the early twentieth century, Ralph Adams Cram and Bertram Goodhue. The architects, William P. Bannister and Richard M. Schell, practiced in Brooklyn and designed a number of Lutheran churches, including St. Luke's, Woodlawn, Queens, and the Church of the Incarnation, Brooklyn. The church retains a watercolor rendering of the building signed by Schell in 1911. Within the church is a mural, *Christ Blessing the Children*, completed in 1914 by the German-born artist C. Paul

Jennewein, who later became a notable sculptor. Jennewein used two or three of Pastor Howard Snyder's daughters as models for the children blessed by Christ.
NYS and NR 1979; HLPC

16. ST. MARY'S ROMAN CATHOLIC CHURCH, SCHOOL, RECTORY AND CONVENT
162 Broadway
1848, 1913, 1922-1924
Patrick C. Keely; Arthur Longyear; Edward F. Fanning

In 1848, St. Mary's Parish, organized in 1835 primarily for Irish immigrant workers on the Delaware and Hudson Canal and their

8

families, erected a large, brick, Gothic Revival church designed by the prolific architect, Patrick C. Keely. This Brooklyn architect was responsible for the plans of some 500 Catholic churches in New York State, not counting his churches in New York City. While the Gothic forms were limited—pointed-arched windows and doors, a scattering of pinnacles, and a richly crocketed spire—St. Mary's seems to have been the first large-scale use of the Gothic Revival in Kingston. Keely's design exemplified the thought, widespread at the time, that Gothic architecture was synonymous with Christian architecture because the great Gothic cathedrals of medieval Europe signaled a golden age for the Christian church.

St. Mary's School (1913), by Arthur C. Longyear, is in the Gothic style to announce the Christian focus of the educational pro-gram, whereas Longyear's Kingston High School (1913-1915) is classical, reflective of secular education. The Gothic cross-mullioned windows of St. Mary's School were arranged in broad bands to admit abundant daylight.

Between 1922 and 1924 the church was much altered. Keely's spire and pinnacles were removed, and the building was wrapped in a more refined Gothic exterior of brick and cast-stone, its style resembling the English Lutheran church on Wurts Street. The renovated Gothic church is harmonious with the Gothic rectory (1923-1924), and convent (1924), all three by Edward F. Fanning, a New York architect. The rectory and convent are especially elegant interpretations of the Gothic, in contrast to the heavy, mid-Victorian Gothic of the former Church of the Holy Spirit on Wurts Street.

NYS and NR 1979

16. St. Mary's Roman Catholic Church and Rectory (vintage photo)

17. THOMAS CORNELL CARRIAGE HOUSE
50 Post Street
1872
J. A. Wood

Although shorn of its stable wing, iron cresting, and other ornamental details, the mansarded, round-arched carriage house of Thomas Cornell (1813-1890) still suggests something of his leading position in Rondout's commercial society of the 1870s. Cornell's residence, across Post Street and facing Wurts Street, was demolished in the early 1940s, but elements of the landscaped grounds survive in the adjoining Cornell Park; note the iron urn cast by J. W. Fiske of New York that once stood in front of the Cornell house and now stands before the Veterans Monument (1943).

J. A. Wood's Second Empire-style design for the carriage house was published in A. J. Bicknell's *Wooden and Brick Buildings* (New York, 1875). The three-part structure included a three-bedroom house in the left wing, carriage storage in the recessed center, and stable in the no-longer-extant right wing. All three were crowned by mansard roofs with intricately detailed dormers and iron cresting. The central carriage entrance was topped with its own very high mansard, or French, roof that sheltered nothing but provided a stylish vertical accent. Those of simpler taste who disliked mansards might find this a prime example of what the *Freeman* (July 16, 1873) called the "French roof epidemic." The stable, according to Wood's drawing, had circular dormers and two circular windows facing Post Street, while the carriage doors were ornamented with concentric circles. Was Wood referring to carriage wheels? A weathervane shown in Wood's drawing took the form of a long-necked bird, similar to those of the bases of the Cornell garden urns.
NYS and NR 1979; HLPC

18. COMMERCIAL BUILDINGS
61, 63, 65, and 101 Broadway
c. 1874

While urban renewal during the 1960s destroyed the east side of Broadway from the Strand to St. Mary's Church, on the west side several commercial buildings with bluestone sills and cast-iron storefronts by the Rondout

17. Thomas Cornell Carriage House (Wood drawing)

18. Commercial Buildings on Broadway

Iron Works survive at 61, 65, and 101 Broadway. As in the case of the nearby West Strand buildings, the Italianate style was employed, usually with bracketed eaves and cast-iron arched lintels on the upper stories. For much of the twentieth century, 101 Broadway was occupied by the Rehrer Bakery.

Of special interest is 63 Broadway, with the date 1874 incised in the stone sill, piers, also dated 1874, made by the Excelsior Iron Works of Kingston, and highly ornamental metal brackets at the cornice. The Excelsior Iron Works expanded its Union Avenue (Broadway) foundry in 1870 with plans by a proprietor, Robert H. Shultis. (*Kingston Journal,* July 13, 1870)
NYS and NR 1979; HLPC

19. JEWISH COMMUNITY CENTER (Kingston Community Development) 97 Broadway 1925 Gerard W. Betz

The Jewish Community Center was a remodeling of Mann's Hall, a brick building with garage on the first floor and dance hall above. The garage was transformed into a library, meeting rooms, and gymnasium; the dance hall was altered to allow stage performances. The new Georgian-Federal façade with brick arches and keystones suggests that the Jewish Community Center was to look like other American institutions that had chosen the same style, for example, the YMCA (by Jackson and Rosencrans, 1912; destroyed by fire 1991) on Broadway. The Jewish

8

Community Center then had none of the exotic touches such as those that distinguished the cupola of Temple Emanuel on Abeel Street, which had been built more than a generation earlier when assimilation was apparently less desired.

Similarly, the Knights of Columbus building at 389 Broadway had been designed by Charles S. Keefe in the "colonial style" of Congress Hall in Philadelphia. At the cornerstone laying in 1913, District Attorney William D. Cunningham strongly defended Roman Catholics against slanderous attacks that labeled them as unpatriotic. By adopting American colonial or Georgian architectural forms, Jews and Catholics could demonstrate that they were entirely devoted to American ideals.

NYS and NR 1979; HLPC

County quarries, as well as the sawing, rubbing, and planing of the rough stone, and the loading of cut and uncut stone onto river boats. With its bluestone walls, the office building of course served to advertise the Fitches' product. Avoiding the utilitarian appearance of other creekside buildings associated with the bluestone and cement industries, J. A. Wood added such modish touches as the polychrome arches and mansard roof with iron crest. The cupola, with finial and flag pole, was certainly meant to be eye-catching. The *Kingston Journal* (1870) called it the finest office in the county. In 1972 the long-abandoned building was restored (without the original window frames and iron shutters) and transformed into a residence by James and Alice Berardi.

HLPC

19. Jewish Community Center

20. SIMEON AND WILLIAM B. FITCH OFFICE
540 Abeel Street
1870
J. A. Wood

The office of the Fitches, wholesale dealers in North River bluestone, was originally surrounded by the clamor and bustle of wagons unloading bluestone brought from Ulster

20. Simeon and William B. Fitch Office

21. THOMAS J. FEENEY ENTERPRISES
613 Abeel Street
1866, c. 1950

Bernard Feeney, his wife, Bridget Knox Feeney, and their three sons operated canal boats on the Delaware and Hudson Canal, and their descendants have been engaged in boat building along the Rondout Creek for nearly a century. Three Quonset huts, one painted yellow with "FEENEY RELIANCE MARINE" in bold letters, have been prominent in the industrial landscape of Abeel Street since about 1950. Quonset huts—portable, prefabricated huts of half-cylindrical shape with corrugated metal exteriors—were mass produced during World War II. The Navy alone obtained some 153,000, and many were sold after the war to serve civilian commercial and industrial purposes.

Another Quonset hut, at 18 Downs Street, was used by Walter Smith Welding Supplies, and about 1949 two huts were joined for the Martin-Moran auto dealership at 450 East Chester Street (since 1965 operated as De Micco Motors). All these huts survive, but several near the Rondout Creek, used for storage by the city's Department of Public Works in 1951, do not.

Also on the Feeney property is a small, stone-fronted office dated 1866 in the window lintel. It probably belonged to one of the bluestone yards of the area.

21. Thomas J. Feeney Enterprises

22. SWEENEY HOUSE-FATHER DIVINE PEACE MISSION
67 Chapel Street
c. 1870

In the city, but in what seems a rural setting, the Sweeney house is a good example of the Second Empire-style house with mansard roof and paired brackets at the eaves. At least as interesting as the house are its past owners. When pictured by De Lisser in 1896, it was the home of Mrs. Elizabeth E. Sweeney of the bluestone firm, E. Sweeney and Son. Oddly, the house is built of wood. In the mid-twentieth century it served as a peace mission of Father Divine, the charismatic Black utopian evangelist.

22. Sweeney House-Father Divine Peace Mission

23. MOUNT ZION CEMETERY
South Wall Street
c. 1840 and later

This African-American cemetery is scarcely visible from South Wall Street

23. Mount Zion Cemetery

because it is set well back from the street in a semi-rural setting. Little is known about the history of the cemetery, although Gail Schneider discovered a deed dated May 1, 1840, between Henry and Ann Houghtaling, parties of the first part, and Richard Peterson, Samuel Brown, and Samuel Beekman, Trustees of the "Coulered People's Burying Ground," parties of the second part. What is apparent is the beauty of the setting, a wooded, elevated tongue of land extending from the cemetery entrance on South Wall Street and providing views down the steep slope towards the Rondout Creek.

While smaller than Montrepose and Wiltwyck cemeteries, and lacking their grand monuments and mausolea, Mount Zion is apparently older. Its landscape features are as appealingly picturesque as those found at Montrepose and Wiltwyck, which probably were originally intended for the burial of white Kingstonians. Community efforts to remove overgrown nature have revealed numbers of gravestones from the second half of the nineteenth century to the 1980s, often marking the graves of Civil War and World War veterans. Some Civil War gravestones were probably lost in May 1918 when vandals took some twenty-six monuments from the graves of Civil War soldiers and hurled them down the embankment, while ruining fifteen other markers. Many in the Kingston community were outraged by this vandalism. Sadly, the graves of most of Kingston's nineteenth-century African-American population are now unmarked.

TOUR 9:
PONCKHOCKIE

I n the late nineteenth century, many of Ponckhockie's houses were occupied by workers, owners, and managers of the nearby cement and brick industries. Most unusual is the concrete structure of the Children's Church, erected for the families of the Newark Lime and Cement Manufacturing Company. The church stands today within sight of the abandoned cement mines.

Newark Lime and Cement Manufacturing Company
(lithograph, *County Atlas of Ulster*, 1875)

TOUR 9:
PONCKHOCKIE

1. **CHILDREN'S CHURCH, OR UNION CHAPEL**
   (Ponckhockie Congregational Church)
2. **NEWARK LIME AND CEMENT MANUFACTURING COMPANY**
3. **DAVID GILL HOUSE**
4. **EDWARD TOMPKINS HOUSE**
   (Children's Home of Kingston)
5. **UNION FREE SCHOOL, DISTRICT NO. 13**
   (later District No. 4)
6. **JOHN H. CORDTS HOUSE**
7. **JOHN N. CORDTS HOSE COMPANY**

9

1. Children's Church, or Union Chapel (lithograph, *County Atlas of Ulster*, 1875)

1. CHILDREN'S CHURCH, OR UNION CHAPEL (Ponckhockie Congregational Church)
93 Abruyn Street
1870
J. A. Wood

Gothic Revival churches with pointed arches, tracery, buttresses, and steeple are common, but this is a rare and early example of concrete construction applied to a Gothic church. It is surely worth a detour. The Newark Lime and Cement Manufacturing Co. paid for its construction as a non-sectarian Sunday School, and more generally to make "liberal provision for the moral and intellectual improvement of [its] employees," while demonstrating the practicality of the concrete church. Nineteenth-century architects were usually reluctant to deviate from traditional materials, especially when designing churches.

Calvin Tomkins and James G. Lindsley, officials of the cement company, were apparently responsible for commissioning this paternalistic institution. Its walls consist of local natural cement combined with crushed bluestone, and finished with cement stucco scored to imitate stone blocks. The tower base displays a quatrefoil panel with the construction date 1870 cast in concrete. The church is perhaps the oldest surviving example of a reinforced concrete building in America: there are simple iron reinforcing plates and rods in the buttresses and, originally, in the 150-foot-high steeple (damaged by weathering, the upper portion was removed in 1965). The view of the church published in Beers's 1875 *Atlas* shows the steeple and surrounding pinnacles intact, and a cement mine's horizontal shaft looming mysteriously in the distance.
NYS and NR 1980; HLPC

2. NEWARK LIME AND CEMENT MANUFACTURING COMPANY
Union Street
c. 1870

This building, once a mule barn, later a church, and now a ruin, appears in an 1875 lithograph of "Newark Lime & Cement Manufacturing Co.'s Works, Rondout" in Beers's *County Atlas of Ulster*. "The largest manufacturing establishment in the City of Kingston" (Sylvester, 1880), this enterprise extended from Rondout Creek wharves to partway up the hill known as the Vleightbergh (Hasbrouck Park Hill), which was honeycombed with tunnels for extracting the stone from which cement was made. In 1871 there were twenty-one kilns, two mill buildings, four storehouses, and various shops, stables and barns, including the now derelict mule barn. Two buildings stand out in the lithograph as having architectural embellishment: the mule barn set back into the Vleightbergh, and the company store. The store, which stands on the East Strand at

2. Newark Lime and Cement Manufacturing Company

Tomkins Street, has been much altered, but was originally a bracketed Italianate building dated 1868 in the cornice.

Not surprisingly, the walls of both buildings are of concrete. The windows and central doorway of the mule barn are distinguished by a projecting decorative molding, mixing elements of the classical pediment with the Gothic drip molding. Rising above the gable roof was a narrow clerestory. Overall, the design somewhat resembled a church. Remarkably, after the closing of the cement works, the barn was acquired by an African-American congregation, Emanuel Baptist Church, as a 1926 cornerstone inserted in the earlier concrete wall testifies. In 1927 the Rev. C. H. King led an effort to transform the barn into a more dignified Gothic church, following designs by Augustus R. Schrowang. While the interior was altered for religious and social functions, the exterior never received the traceried Gothic windows Schrowang proposed.

3. DAVID GILL HOUSE
54 Gill Street
1869
David Gill?

Carpenter and builder David Gill (1823-1910) erected this house for his own family. Gill accomplished a virtuoso performance with the Italianate paired brackets supporting the projecting eaves, as well as the turned balusters and pendants of the second-story porch. The porch and cupola provided views of Rondout Creek.

In 1896 Gill was described as having "done more, perhaps, than any other man in adding to ... [Rondout's] growth in the way of buildings. ... He began by building houses and selling them, and then purchased lots on each side of the street, which he graded, and put up pretty residences, which met with a ready sale." (*Commemorative Biographical*

Record, 139) Gill's own, highly ornamented house surely helped boost these sales.

3. David Gill House

4. EDWARD TOMPKINS HOUSE
(Children's Home of Kingston)
Grove Street
1870

Calvert Vaux designed the Walter B. Crane house (1862-1863), which stood next to the Tompkins house on Grove Street, both houses overlooking Rondout Creek and the Hudson River. The Tompkins house is a picturesque Gothic Revival design of the kind Vaux produced, but the architect of this house is unknown. The Gothic and picturesque notes are clear in the complex framing of the gable of the porch facing Grove Street, and the gable directly above this porch emerging from the roof. Other gables sheltering the dormer windows are similarly enriched with Gothic motifs. The delightful balcony jutting out from the roof of the south façade, and the chimney with attached Gothic dovecote, are strikingly unusual picturesque features.

While the ornament of the Tompkins house is old-fashioned and complex, the wall surfaces and windows are quite plain because of the concrete walls. The innovative use of concrete here—like its use at the Children's Church and Union Free School—

4. Edward Tompkins House (vintage photo)

was tied to the local cement industry. Edward Tompkins was an official of the Newark Lime and Cement Manufacturing Co., whose works were a short walk from his home.

5. UNION FREE SCHOOL, DISTRICT NO. 13 (later District No. 4)
229 Delaware Avenue
1867

Free public education for all—including the children of immigrants and the working class—was a movement that produced this school, built of concrete apparently supplied at low cost by the Newark Lime and Cement Manufacturing Company. The company

undoubtedly viewed supporting the education of its employees' children as a wise investment to secure a stable labor force. The Children's Church, a few blocks away on Abruyn Street, was another paternalistic gesture by the company.

The design adheres to the picturesque taste of the 1860s in the segmental-arched windows, broad overhang of the complex hipped roof, and vertical accents of chimneys and cupola. Taxpayers were cajoled into supporting new school construction by arguments citing improved student health through adequate space, heat, and ventilation. (Was the latter enhanced by the cupola?) It was also important to promise no "unnecessary expenditures for show and ornament." (Kingston

9

5. Union Free School, District No. 13 (vintage photo)

Board of Education, *8th Annual Report,* 1871) In 1898 Kingston architect Charles E. Hillyer added the section of the school farthest from Delaware Avenue, also with concrete walls and cupola.

6. JOHN H. CORDTS HOUSE
132 Lindsley Avenue
1873

Brick manufacturer John H. Cordts built his brick, mansarded, Second Empire-style house on a hill overlooking his brickyard and a panorama of the Hudson River. While houses of the Victorian era frequently had towers purely for picturesque compositional effect, Miss Florence Cordts reported that her grandfather set up a telescope in the tower to keep track of shipping on the river.

Cordts's status as a leading Rondout businessman found expression in this prominently sited and highly visible house. The *Daily Freeman* (April 21 and July 11, 1874) reported that it was the largest private residence in the city and environs, and some visitors were said to have mistaken it for the new city hall! Mansard roofs, according to the *Freeman* (September 16, 1872), gave houses an "aristocratic air," and this example's concave surfaces, iron cresting, bracketed eaves, as well as the richly decorated windows of the tower's mansard, increased that aura. The grounds are also graced with a mansarded stable-carriage house, and delightful gazebo full of jigsaw

6. John H. Cordts House

cutouts. The gazebo, tower, broad porch, and tower balcony all tell of the significance of the view.
HLPC

7. JOHN N. CORDTS HOSE COMPANY
211 Delaware Avenue
c. 1894

This and the similarly designed Union Hose Company at 216 East Union Street, are remarkably well-preserved nineteenth-century firehouses continuing to serve their original function with volunteer firefighters. Both are segmental-arched, brick buildings with decoratively shaped panels for the name of the company, and both have brackets, which support the top cornice, with simple Neo-Grec fluting. This hose company was named for New York State Senator John Nicholas Cordts (1865-1913), son of John H. Cordts and president of the hose company from its organization until his death.

7. John N. Cordts Hose Company

9

MILL ST. LOOKING TOWARD BROADWAY   PICT TAKEN FEB 6

Demolition of Rondout Savings Bank, 1969.

LOST KINGSTON

Kingston has lost its share of historic architecture, most famously in the burning of the town by the British in 1777. Eighteenth-century stone buildings continued to be destroyed in the nineteenth and twentieth centuries. In 1907, Edgar Mayhew Bacon noted in *The Hudson River* that "commercial Kingston has nearly swallowed the quaint, historic town that used to sit comfortably on the site of old Wiltwyck." Nevertheless, since the 1880s the veneration of Kingston's old stone houses has grown to a point where continued losses, unless by accident, seem unlikely. Kingstonians can rightly take pride in their successful preservation of many stone houses in the uptown area, and the designation of historic districts, including nineteenth-century landmarks, in various parts of the city (see the list on page 14).

Many of the city's finest nineteenth-century buildings, however, were destroyed before preservation sentiment for the Victorian era arose in the 1960s and 1970s. Whole blocks of well designed commercial buildings and houses were demolished in Rondout by advocates of urban renewal in the 1960s. The adjacent photo documents the February 1969 demolition of the Rondout Savings Bank, which had stood since 1928 on Broadway at Mill Street.

Independent of urban renewal, three noteworthy houses by Calvert Vaux, the important New York architect with family ties to Rondout, have disappeared: his houses for Walter Crane, Albert Terry, and Samuel Coykendall. Particularly regrettable is the loss of the hilltop studio in Rondout that Vaux designed for his brother-in-law, the Hudson River School painter Jervis McEntee. Calvert Vaux's son, Downing Vaux, was responsible for the festive architecture of Kingston Point Park and Boat Landing, which now must be envisioned by way of vintage postcards. Similarly, all of Kingston's railroad passenger stations—the West Shore, Ontario and Western, and Ulster and Delaware—have been destroyed, as have all four of the breweries that flourished in 1900: Hoffman, Cummings, Hauck, and Barmann.

Many Kingstonians express dismay at the destruction of the classical post office (1904) on Broadway, designed by James Knox Taylor. While its style derived from the European Renaissance, in 1904 it was called "distinctly colonial in keeping with our colonial city and its traditions." Was the cupola thought to hark back to the 1818 courthouse? At the other end of the architectural spectrum, vintage diners have not fared well in the city. Some have been destroyed; others have been moved away, as lunch wagons and diners are by definition constructed off-site, and so are easily moved. In 1912 the *Freeman* reported that "the lunch wagon of Richard Ryan on Broadway near the West Shore crossing was removed from its foundations this morning and loaded on one of the trucks of Emerson Powell and taken to Saugerties where it was set up on Partition Street." Other intriguing, but inherently ephemeral sites include the Aerodrome, a 1912 open-air theater for motion pictures and vaudeville on O'Reilly Street near Broadway.

Twentieth-century alterations intended to improve the appearance of nineteenth-century Victorian buildings have also essentially destroyed those buildings. Richard M. Upjohn's First National Bank (1862-1863) on Wall Street, a Ruskinian polychrome Gothic design by a talented architect (son of the more famous Richard Upjohn), was cloaked in a severe, monochrome Renaissance shell in 1947. J. A. Wood's Ulster County Savings Bank, even more exuberantly ornamented than Upjohn's bank, was toned down with a new brick exterior by Harry Halverson in the 1950s.

Then too, some twentieth-century preservation efforts were, with twenty-first-century hindsight, misguided. The removal of the ground-story façade of 9 Hone Street (c. 1840) in 1935, by local antiques dealer Fred J. Johnston, for sale to the distinguished collector Henry F. du Pont, followed standards accepted at the time. The surviving building and the community, however, are the poorer for this act of preservation; the triple-arched glassy storefront with Ionic columns fronting the recessed doorway was incorporated into "Shop Lane" at du Pont's Winterthur Museum in Delaware.

Even as this guide was being prepared, the Brigham School (by Arthur C. Longyear, 1899-1901), significant remnants of the Kingston Hotel (where the artist John Vanderlyn died in 1852), the former Powell, Smith, & Co. cigar factory on Broadway, and the Kingston City Laboratory and Ulster County Tumor Clinic were all demolished. And there are many endangered buildings. The Tudor Revival Kirkland Hotel and adjoining buildings on Clinton Avenue, said to have made strangers think they were near Shakespeare's home, are falling into terminal decay. Vandals have damaged Solomon D. Burger's residence (c. 1872 and 1880s, according to George Allen's research) at 107 Henry Street. Burger was a leading contractor and builder; his house has some of the Victorian quirkiness of Philadelphia architect Frank Furness. The former Ulster County Academy on West Chestnut Street, Kingston Consolidated Railway car barn on Broadway, and Forst meat packing plant on Abeel Street, all need new uses to survive as emblems of Kingston's historic architecture and culture.

The preservation picture is not altogether bleak. Thanks to historic preservation activists like the late Fred J. Johnston and the Friends of Historic Kingston, and to the unheralded efforts of property owners who thoughtfully maintain their buildings, much of pre-1950 Kingston is intact, helping make it a desirable place to live and visit. The city government's commitment to preservation brought about the excellent restoration of city hall (by John G. Waite Associates), and Ulster County is restoring the Matthewis Persen house at Crown and John Streets after completion of a thorough investigation of the structure (by Kenneth Hewes Barricklo). Remarkably, bits of Kingston Point Park also are re-emerging, with broad community support led by the Rotary Club.

Old Dutch Church, Wall and Main Streets, 1752 (burned by the British 1777).

**Kingston Hotel, Crown Street, site of John Vanderlyn's death in 1852
(destroyed in stages, the last in 2000).**

**Wall Street, about 1830, including the tower of Old Dutch Church, Ulster County
Courthouse, shops of J. S. Smith, L. M. Osterhoudt, and a printing office.**

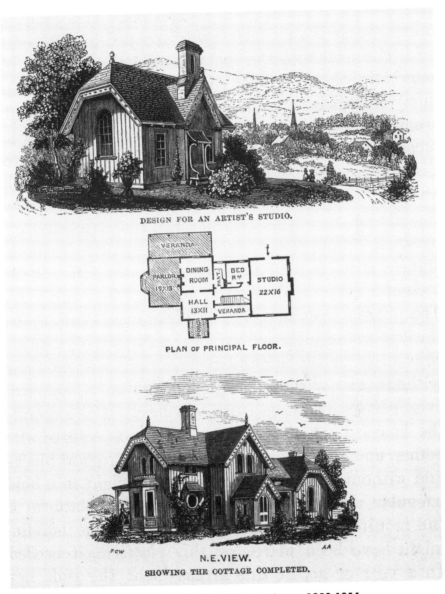

DESIGN FOR AN ARTIST'S STUDIO.

PLAN OF PRINCIPAL FLOOR.

N.E. VIEW.
SHOWING THE COTTAGE COMPLETED.

**Jervis McEntee Studio, West Chestnut Street, 1853-1854,
Calvert Vaux and Frederick Withers.**

Walter B. Crane House, Grove Street, 1862-1863, Calvert Vaux.

First National Bank of Kingston, Wall Street at John Street, 1862-1864, Richard M. Upjohn (reconstructed 1947).

Ulster County Savings Bank, 280 Wall Street, 1868-1869, J. A. Wood
(altered in 1950s by Harry Halverson).

William Van Aken House, 249 Washington Avenue, 1870,
Edward Brink (destroyed by fire, 1998).

**Kingston Argus, Wall Street adjacent to the courthouse,
1874, J. A. Wood (demolished 1913).**

**Cornell Building, Ferry Street at Broadway, 1881-1883,
J. A. Wood? (demolished 1966).**

West Shore Railroad Depot (Union Depot), Railroad Avenue, 1882-1883.

Kingston Academy, Academy Green, 1830-1831, Henry Rector,
altered 1883 by Charles W. Romeyn (demolished 1916).

**Albert Terry House, 293 Broadway, 1885,
Calvert Vaux (demolished 1970s).**

**Samuel Coykendall House, West Chestnut Street, begun 1890,
Calvert Vaux (demolished 1949).**

Powell, Smith and Company, Broadway at Pine Grove Avenue,
completed 1891 (demolished 1999).

Kingston City Hospital, Broadway, 1892-1894, Charles W. Romeyn
(destroyed by fire 1926).

Kingston Point Park, 1893-1897, Downing Vaux (closed as an amusement center 1931).

Andrew F. Mason House, 15 Downs Street, Andrew F. Mason, c. 1893 (much altered).

Peckham Manufacturing Company (Peckham Motor Truck and Wheel Company),
Hasbrouck Street near Grand Street, 1890s (partially destroyed).

Brigham School, 107 O'Neil Street, 1899-1901, Arthur Curtis Longyear
(demolished 2000).

Kingston Savings Bank, 273 Wall Street, 1900 (reconstructed 1960).

New York, Ontario and Western Railway Station, Fair Street extension, 1902,
Jackson, Rosencrans and Canfield.

Post Office, Broadway at Prince Street, 1904-1908, James Knox Taylor (demolished December 1969-January 1970).

Quick Lunch, Railroad Avenue near West Shore Railroad Depot, c. 1910.

Barmann's Brewery, Barmann Avenue (demolished 1945).

Young Men's Christian Association, 507 Broadway, 1912, Jackson and Rosencrans (destroyed by fire July and November 1991).

Ulster County Tuberculosis Hospital, Golden Hill, completed 1931,
Teller and Halverson with Charles S. Keefe.

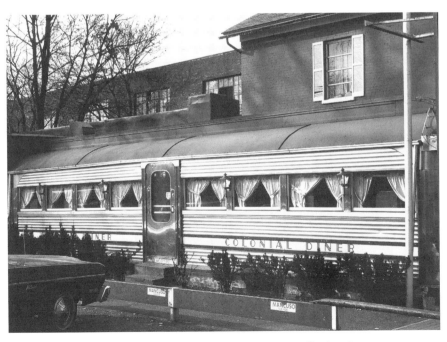

Colonial Diner, 713 Broadway, late 1940s, a Silk City Diner
made by Paterson Vehicle Co. (removed 1985).

Charles S. Keefe (1876-1946) in 1905.

SOME NOTABLE KINGSTON BUILDERS
AND ARCHITECTS

J. (JOHN) A. WOOD (1837-1910)

J. A. Wood was the leading architect in the Mid-Hudson region in the late 1860s and 1870s, designing several of Kingston's most prominent buildings of that period. Born in 1837 in the Town of Bethel, Sullivan County, he was the son of Stephen C. Wood and Mary Crist Wood. By 1863 he was practicing in Poughkeepsie, where his office remained until 1871 when he established his office on Broadway in New York. His operations were centered in New York for the rest of his life.

His buildings in Kingston include: First Baptist Church, Albany Avenue, 1868; conversion of former Dutch Reformed Church to St. Joseph's Roman Catholic Church, 1869; Kingston Music Hall (later Opera House), on Fair Street, 1867-1869; Ulster County Savings Bank, Wall Street, 1868-1869; Office of Simeon and William B. Fitch, Wilbur, 1870; Children's Church, Ponckhockie, 1870-1871; Kingston City Alms House, 1872-1874; Thomas Cornell Carriage House, 1873; Dr. Robert Loughran House, Fair Street, 1873; Kingston Argus Building, Wall Street, 1874 (demolished); First Presbyterian Church, Elmendorf Street, 1878; New York State Armory, Broadway, 1878; and Stuyvesant Hotel, John and Fair Streets, 1910.

Wood became something of a specialist in hotel design, and was responsible for the second Overlook Mountain House (1878) above Woodstock, the Tremper House (1879) in Phoenicia, the Grand Hotel (1881) at Highmount, as well as hotels in Georgia and Florida. The most famous of the latter is the Tampa Bay Hotel (1891), preserved by the University of Tampa.

J. A. Wood died in Middletown on December 18, 1910, and was buried in Evergreen Cemetery, Town of Bethel. His career has been the subject of intense and fruitful research by Annon Adams and James Storrow, who have generously shared their findings with me.

ALBERT MAUTERSTOCK (1851-1923)

Albert Mauterstock's career is representative of the nineteenth-century practice of carpenters and builders who would, on occasion, assume the role and title of "architect" with little or no architectural training. Mauterstock was primarily, as his 1898 billhead announced, a "contractor, manufacturer and builder." At his "factory" at 7-9 Spring Street his workers did "turning, planing, sawing, &c. All kinds of stair work and hard wood floors. Door, sash and blinds. Window and door frames. Picture frames ..." His "office and sales-rooms" were at 89-93 Broadway.

Mauterstock was a native of Rondout, the son of a ship and house builder, Levi Mauterstock, and Sarah A. Overbagh Mauterstock. His schooling ended at age fifteen when he left the Kingston Academy. He became a carpenter by working for Isaac Burhans and Stephen D. Mills for four years. In 1872 he began his own building business, and in 1883 he married Joanna F. Cothing. By 1896 he could boast of the success of his enterprise, which occupied 11,000 square feet, exclusive of his lumberyards. No doubt his contacts as a Mason, Methodist, sergeant in the militia, and Republican served him well.

The *Commemorative Biographical Record of Ulster County* (1896) provides a list of buildings Mauterstock erected in Rondout, including the house of brick manufacturer Albert Terry on Broadway (1886, designed by Calvert Vaux; destroyed in the 1970s) and Mrs. James Van Deusen's house on West Chestnut Street (1891). In Stone Ridge he built the elegant Francis H. Leggett house, and in New Paltz the Academy (1885, designed by Charles Romeyn; destroyed by fire in 1906).

The *Biographical Record* clearly distinguishes buildings Mauterstock designed as "architect," notably the Conrad Hiltebrant house in Rondout. He is said to have "planned and built" other structures, such as the "mercantile house" of Stock and Cordts, and there, too, he probably acted as designer. In New Paltz his name appeared as "Architect" on the plaque commemorating those responsible for the 1888 Ulster County Home.

Albert Mauterstock died in 1923 and is buried in Montrepose Cemetery.

ARTHUR CURTIS LONGYEAR (1867-1929)

Arthur Longyear was apparently of a Kingston family. He first appeared as an architect in New York directories in 1890 at 247 Broadway, and last appeared in 1909 at 126 Liberty Street. Beginning in 1908 he was listed in Kingston directories as an architect residing at 66 East Chester Street, with no separate office address.

In Kingston he designed the George J. Smith house (c. 1893) on West Chestnut Street, but his specialty was school design: Brigham School (1899-1901) on O'Neil Street, St. Peter's School (1911) on Adams Street, St. Joseph's School (1912) on Wall Street, St. Mary's School (1913) on Broadway, and Kingston High School (1913-1915), the latter representing the culmination of his career.

Longyear died in Kingston Hospital, November 3, 1929, and is buried in Wiltwyck Cemetery.

MYRON S. TELLER (1875-1959) AND HARRY HALVERSON (1891-1988)

In 1913 when many wealthy Americans looked to Europe for guidance in all cultural matters, including the design of their great houses, Kingston's Myron S. Teller was praised by C. Matlack Price, a prominent architectural critic, for designing the Ulster County residence of Jules Breuchaud as a "convincing example of true American architecture ... a country house ... perfectly appropriate to its immediate locality." This was so because Teller made the house an adaptation of the old Dutch stone and clapboarded farmhouses of the region.

Kingston's leading architect in the early twentieth century, Myron Steadman Teller was the son of George Teller, a genealogist and, among other positions, Supreme Court Librarian of Ulster County. Little is known about Myron's architectural training, but it probably began in Kingston architectural offices, as was the case with his contemporary, Charles Keefe. The 1899 Kingston Directory lists Teller as an architect in New York with residence in his parental home at 169 Washington Avenue. It was probably at this time that he attended Cooper Union. By 1900 he established his office in Kingston, where his practice would be centered for the remainder of his career.

An early Teller design (c. 1902) was a proposal for a concrete building for the newly founded Benedictine Hospital; the design was rejected as unsafe, and a New York architect was hired to design a conventional brick and limestone structure. In 1904 he was more successful in executing a routine design for a combined house and store for John L. Salzmann on Sycamore Street. Teller's later work included many buildings that were competent or handsome, but not much different from buildings with similar functions rising in other American cities: his Burgevin Building at the corner of Fair and Main Streets (c. 1904), Central Fire Station (1908) on East O'Reilly Street, James Millard & Son Building (c. 1925) on Prince Street facing Broadway, and Jacobson Shirt Factory (c. 1925) on Cornell Street, belong to this category of his production. The Millard Building's white and freely-classical façade originally was in harmony with the adjacent, but now demolished, classical post office (1904). The Burgevin Building is an example of the eighteenth-century Georgian applied to an early-twentieth-century commercial building, and Teller also used the Georgian for the red-brick DeWitt Roosa house at 212 Fair Street. These were Georgian or Colonial Revival designs that made no specific reference to Kingston's distinctive history.

Teller's first notable commission relating to the city's historic architecture was the "restoration" (actually the improvement) of the Sleight-Tappen House for the Wiltwyck Chapter of the Daughters of the American Revolution in 1907. While not historically accurate, Teller's work was sufficiently admired that he was called upon to design other, more accurate, restorations of the Van Keuren house on Green Street for Mrs. W. Anderson Carl, the Van Buren house, also on Green Street, for Mrs. Mae K. Gordon, and the Johannes Masten house on Pearl Street for Annie E. P. Searing. By 1929 these and other stone-house restorations led the historian Helen Wilkinson Reynolds to recommend him as a member of the Holland Society—hence, connected by blood to the

Dutch colonists of the Hudson Valley—with special expertise in the restoration of the early stone houses of the region.

Teller's ambition as a restoration architect was to remove nineteenth and early-twentieth-century alterations and additions, replace lost Colonial surfaces and moldings, and "camouflage the modern rooms and conveniences to harmonize with the spirit of the original style." Sometimes this meant cannibalizing derelict Colonial houses and barns for their old beams, woodwork, and hardware. Camouflaging also required finding workers who could imitate Colonial craftsmanship and forms, particularly the hand-forged iron hardware.

Teller had difficulty finding new hardware in historically correct patterns for his restorations, and so he collected old hardware and had it reproduced by Ulster County blacksmiths, especially men of the Van Kleeck family who were of Hudson Valley Dutch ancestry and had been blacksmiths in rural Samsonville for three generations. Presumably the spirit of Colonial craftsmen survived in these men. It was fortunate that the Van Kleeck blacksmith shop was a rustic wooden building in a lovely rural setting, as Teller used pictures of it in articles publicizing his enterprise.

When other Colonial Revival architects learned of the high quality of the hardware being made for Teller and sought it for their own clients, the production of hand-wrought hardware in colonial patterns became a business for Teller. He set up a shop and sales room on Washington Avenue and employed several men to hammer out and finish the hardware. A reporter found only one "machine" in the shop, and that was rarely used.

At the Philadelphia Sesqui-Centennial International Exposition of 1926, Teller set up a blacksmith shop where his men reproduced colonial hardware, which was used in reconstructing the Colonial-style High Street at the Exposition. The shop provided an educational exhibit for the Exposition's crowds, and advertised Teller's wares. Eventually his hardware was selected for the restoration of George Washington's birthplace at Wakefield, Virginia, the Jumel Mansion in New York, and Washington Irving's Sunnyside in Tarrytown. It was also chosen for wholly new Colonial buildings: the Franklin D. Roosevelt Library in Hyde Park, and buildings by Kingston architect Charles Keefe and Philadelphia architect R. Brognard Okie.

Teller's commitment to Colonial forms and craftsmanship was rooted, it seems, in his belief in the importance of ancestral tradition. He was a member of the Holland Society, which, through Helen Reynolds, recommended his restoration talents. He sought out craftsmen of Hudson Valley Dutch ancestry. And he was very pleased to be commissioned to restore the eighteenth-century Schoonmaker house in Accord, because, as he wrote in 1939, the property was "one of the early American grants with a homestead lived in by a descendant as it was handed down through the generations and exemplifies the homeing instinct of the Ulster County Dutch folk."

Teller was a man of the twentieth century, however. He traveled to old stone houses by automobile. He apparently saw no incongruity in designing the Senate Garage (1921) on North Front Street in antique Dutch style for John Van Kleeck. His Wiltwyck

Inn (c. 1910) on Main Street had patrons who arrived by auto, but its Dutch stepped gables made perfect sense since it stood across from the ancient churchyard of Old Dutch Church. In 1928 his firm designed a highly ornamental gas station in Dutch style for the Newcombe Oil Co. Plans for this were signed by Harry Halverson. In 1926 Teller formed a partnership with Harry Halverson, and thereafter Teller devoted much time to his hardware business and Colonial house restorations.

Teller was the most prominent architect in the area between the world wars. In 1927 he headed the architectural commission responsible for the rebuilding of city hall. Then, in 1941, he was the first president of the Mid-Hudson Valley Architectural Society, comprised of architects from Kingston, Poughkeepsie, and Newburgh. The society organized a tri-city architectural exhibition, which opened to the public in July 1941 in the Municipal Auditorium (the former Armory).

Teller's years of study of the old stone houses of his county culminated in a modest booklet, *The Early Stone Houses of Ulster County, New York*. Teller prepared drawings for the booklet in 1958, and the Ulster County Historical Society published it in 1959, the year of his death.

Teller's long-time partner, Harry Halverson, was born in 1891 in Brooklyn, of Norwegian immigrant parents, Louis and Aldina Olson Halverson. The family soon moved to Kingston, where his father was a building contractor. In 1911 Harry graduated from Kingston Academy, and in 1917 he received a degree in architecture from Syracuse University. He then worked in several architectural offices, including that of the State Architect in Albany, and served in the Army Corps of Engineers in World War I. In 1984 he explained that because of the war he did not make the customary postgraduate architectural tour of Europe, and in fact had never toured Europe, but enjoyed several visits to Colonial Williamsburg.

The partnership of Teller and Halverson continued Teller's focus on Colonial restorations and new Colonial Revival designs in both Dutch and Georgian veins, including the Matthews house (1937-1938) on Charlotte Street and MacKinnon house (1934) on North Manor Avenue. There were also a scattering of buildings in other styles, such as the English half-timbered house of William Fuller near St. John's Church. Halverson was best known in his lifetime for Georgian Revival institutional designs, including Myron J. Michael Junior High School (1934-1938), Ulster County Tuberculosis Hospital (1931, Charles Keefe, Associate Architect; mostly demolished), and Kingston City Laboratory (1935-1940; demolished).

In 1944 the Teller and Halverson partnership ended, with Halverson continuing the practice alone or with associates until his retirement in 1970. During this busy period the firm designed the Ulster County Tumor Clinic (1948-1949; demolished), George Washington School (1950), Old Dutch Church Parish Hall (1951), additions to Kingston Hospital, and several financial institutions, including the Rondout National Bank (1952) and Home-Seekers' Savings and Loan Association (1957). Halverson served on the board of directors of Home-Seekers' and was active in civic groups, including the

Kiwanis Club. Long-gestating plans for an Ulster County office building, conceived by Halverson in the 1940s as a massive Georgian Revival building on a Main Street site formerly occupied by the Eagle Hotel, were never carried out. Instead, the present modern, International Style structure was built in 1963-1964 following plans by Augustus R. Schrowang, Sr., and Augustus R. Schrowang, Jr. Halverson's own late work included schools in the modern idiom.

Harry Halverson died October 26, 1988, and is buried in Wiltwyck Cemetery.

CHARLES S. KEEFE (1876-1946)

Charles Schoonmaker Keefe was described in 1936 by the *Freeman* as "the quiet, courteous gentleman, better known abroad than at home, who goes about our streets ... [and] whose life has been a part of our city and county." In 1946, when noting Keefe's death, the *Architectural Record* cited him as "a widely known house architect and an authority on Colonial American homes." This Kingstonian was a much-published designer of houses in eighteen states from Maine to California (and others in British Columbia and Ecuador), and was one of a number of American architects who specialized in the Colonial Revival and had a wide following between the two world wars.

Charles Keefe was born in Kingston, in 1876, to Andrew J. Keefe and Celestina Priscilla Schoonmaker Keefe. He was of Irish and Hudson Valley Dutch ancestry. His formal education ended before graduation from Kingston Academy; by 1895 he was listed as an architectural apprentice. The next dozen years were spent as a draftsman and architect in Kingston, including several years working for Andrew F. Mason on Downs Street. During this period he served in the Spanish-American War, and in 1905 he married Grace Letta de la Montanye.

About 1907 Keefe set out for New York, working for, and eventually in partnership with, Edward Burnett and Alfred Hopkins in the design of country estates, banks, and prisons. Keefe claimed that in planning the Westchester County Penitentiary at Eastview (1917) he had included a secret escape route for his own use, should the need arise!

The winter of 1910-1911 saw Keefe on his first and only European sojourn, following an itinerary given him by Hopkins (who had studied in Paris at the Ecole des Beaux-Arts) that took him from England through France, Belgium, and Germany, to Italy. Italy impressed him as the fount of good architecture, but recent classical buildings in Paris were "rotten." The disdainful Keefe told Hopkins, "No Beaux-Arts for me if this is the result."

Keefe broke his association with Hopkins in 1920 and established his own office in New York, specializing in Colonial Revival suburban and country houses and farm buildings similar to those he had produced earlier with Burnett and Hopkins. Professional recognition came with his election to the American Institute of Architects in 1924 and the Architectural League of New York in 1928. At this time his residences were appearing in esteemed professional journals, including the *American Architect* and *Architectural Record*, and magazines for householders, especially *House Beautiful*. In

1922 he published *The American House,* which highlighted the recent "Colonial style" houses of leading architects such as Delano and Aldrich, and Dwight James Baum. His credentials as a Colonial expert were strengthened when he edited a revised edition of *The Georgian Period* (1923), a collection of photos and measured drawings of early American buildings, widely used as a source book by Colonial Revivalists.

National publicity came with the bronze medals awarded Keefe in the 1931 and 1932 Better Homes in America competitions headed by Ray Lyman Wilbur, Secretary of the Interior under Herbert Hoover. But Keefe's most popular design was probably one for a "Connecticut Yankee Cottage," featured in the June 1933 *Pictorial Review,* which spurred some 200 inquiries, mostly from New York State. He offered to sell Connecticut Yankee plans to all comers for $25, even though he opposed stock plans furnished by lumber dealers.

While Keefe's national reputation in the 1920s depended in part on his New York City address, he never severed his ties to Kingston. In 1911, he had designed a Colonial Revival home on Lucas Avenue, which he and Grace continued to occupy until their deaths. It was called "Lisnaskea" after the Irish home of his ancestors, although Grace Keefe's stationery named it "The Little White House-on-the-Hill." Before the Depression, he spent five days a week in New York and returned to Lucas Avenue for the weekends. In the early 1930s, as jobs for architects disappeared during the Depression, Keefe closed his New York office and retreated to Kingston, using a part of his home as an office. Still, in this decade he gained as clients Lowell Thomas, Thomas E. Dewey, and others whom the renowned broadcaster had enticed to Quaker Hill, Pawling.

Over the course of his fifty-year career, Keefe used several styles. His earliest known work, a house (c. 1900) for his father at 30 Lafayette Street, is a vernacular Queen Anne design. The George A. Winter house (1911) on Johnston Avenue is a one-story bungalow. The Stanley Matthews house (1926) on Lounsbury Place, and Charles Arnold house (1937) on Manor Avenue are in a severe Tudor style. The house and office (1936-1938) of Philip P. Poley, a veterinarian, on Albany Avenue are stucco and half-timbered "Provincial French."

Nevertheless, his greatest enthusiasm was reserved for Colonial architecture, both old and revived. In 1918 he published a photo-illustrated article, "The Development of the American Doorway," in the *American Architect,* using as examples Kingston and Hurley doorways from colonial times through the Greek Revival of the early and mid-nineteenth century. He explained his admiration for wooden Colonial Revival houses in 1926 by calling them "typically American, being developed by the conditions and needs of our climate and our ways of living." Their simplicity enhanced both their "beauty" and "economy." His attachment to old Colonial buildings, especially those of New England, was such that his infrequent holidays were spent driving with his wife through that region, searching out and photographing old houses. He wrote to *House and Garden* that he trained his wife "to keep her eyes open for good ones. Give her hell if she lets any get by. So in self defense she spots them, altho sometimes she gets dizzy trying."

The simplicity of the Keefes' Georgian home was in response to a limited budget and Keefe's own taste—in Italy he had complained that the Baroque was "too coarse and extravagant." His Knights of Columbus Building (1913) on Broadway, and Walter Price house (1922) on Albany Avenue are also plain Georgian, but in brick. The American Legion Building (1922-1926) on West O'Reilly Street, whose design was donated by Keefe, is lighter and more decorative, thanks to its Federal-style portico. He employed a severe type of Federal style for the Francis O'Connor house (1936) on Manor Avenue, and Mortimer Downer house (1938) on Henry Street. During the Depression, Keefe was struggling financially and glad to be commissioned to design modest Cape Cod cottages for Earl and Letha Gedney on Merritt Avenue (1935), and Olive Marsh on Madison Avenue (1939).

Keefe also used the "Dutch Colonial" house type, with gambrel roof and extended dormers, that was popular across the country in the early twentieth century. A good example is his A. B. Shufeldt house (1921) on Johnston Avenue. Yet, he derived little from Ulster County's old Dutch stone houses, even though he did draw them and did restore Nieuw Dorp (c. 1730) in Hurley for Mr. and Mrs. Eugene Morehouse in 1938. Perhaps he was content to let Myron Teller dominate the local revival of the Dutch Colonial.

While Keefe took great pains with his drawings, he was no historical purist in restoration work or in new Colonial houses where, for example, sunrooms abound. "Good designers never slavishly copy a design," he wrote in The American House. The goal should be "beautiful," "charming," and "delightful" houses expressive of the "owner's good taste" and "a pleasure to ourselves, our friends and to the passerby."

In the 1980s, forty years after Keefe's death, clients remembered him as an amiable gentleman who designed functional and pleasing houses. Letha Gedney, wife of newspaper printer Earl Gedney, knew him since 1930 as a neighbor and then as a client: "We all loved him." He enjoyed telling amusing stories, such as his design of the prison escape route, and he would come to check on the improvements the newly married Gedneys were making to their garden, or advise them to take their dog to Dr. Poley, the veterinarian and Keefe client. Olive Marsh, a school teacher, recalled that Keefe was very careful in supervising construction and making certain that her small house was built within budget. As was his custom, he gave his client a present for the newly completed house—in her case, an antique print of Suez. Keefe befriended his younger rival Harry Halverson and admitted to him just one "vicious habit"—book collecting—while advising him "for every new job buy a book."

Still, Keefe could be stirred to anger, a consequence, he thought, of his Irishness. In 1914 he defended himself from the attacks of James F. Dwyer, Rondout businessman and member of the Knights of Columbus building committee. It seems that Dwyer and his friends thought the design, especially the hipped roof, so bad as to be laughable. Keefe responded: "I feel that I am more competent to judge this than you are. . . . If, as you say, anyone laughs at it they only show their ignorance. Do you remember Congress

Hall, part of the Independence Hall Group in Philadelphia? It is one of the best pieces of Colonial Architecture in Philadelphia and has the same sloping roof you say people laugh at."

In 1924, in a letter to *The Architect*, he railed against those in his profession with "soprano voices and spats" who felt building involved going "into some sort of a trance to commune with the Gods." Rather it was "sweat" that produced the best results, according to this plain-talking, middle-class American man who never attended a university, never became a member of an elite club, or achieved the distinction of being named a Fellow of the American Institute of Architects. Instead, he prized his membership in several veterans' societies.

In the 1930s he opposed the rise of modern design and the professional journals "hipped on modern work." He could not understand why the *Architectural Record* and *Architectural Forum* published so many modern houses, when none of his clients wanted their roofs flat or walls barren. The aims and methods of these journals seemed to Keefe, a Republican, to smack of New Deal ideology: "It looks to me as if the magazines were trying to change the homes of the people much in the same way the crowd in Washington is trying to force us into a better life, whatever that is." (Ironically, Franklin Roosevelt shared Keefe's enthusiasm for Colonial architecture.)

Charles Keefe remained loyal to his traditional ideals to the end. He was a member of the Ulster County War Price and Rationing Board No. 2556.1 in 1944, but that same year, when FDR sent him a form letter asking, as a neighbor, for his vote, Keefe turned it over and made notes for a client's shower and tub. In 1946, after the wartime hiatus in civilian construction, normalcy was returning and Keefe had twenty jobs on hand, including the Gerald Gormley house on Lucas Avenue, which resembles Keefe's own house built nearby some thirty-five years before. But the architect did not live to see the Gormley project completed: he died suddenly July 19, 1946, while on a construction supervision trip to Vermont, and was buried in Wiltwyck Cemetery beneath a monument he designed in 1927.

GERARD W. BETZ (1881-1962)

Gerard Betz was a native of Poughkeepsie. He studied at Pratt Institute in Brooklyn, completed a course in architecture at Columbia University, and studied architectural design with the Society of Beaux-Arts Architects in New York. In 1911-1912 he was employed as associate architect by Myron Teller; in June 1912 they announced the partnership of Teller and Betz, which was dissolved that same December. In 1913 he opened his own office, but was associated with Arthur Longyear in designing Kingston High School.

Betz's designs were typical of the eclectic approach of most early-twentieth-century architects: an Arts and Crafts bungalow (c. 1910) for Ralph Gregory on Manor Avenue; Tudor for his own house (c. 1928) on Pearl Street; severely abstracted ornament applied to the Manhattan Shirt Factory (1919) on Hoffman Street, and Mohican Market (1926-

1927) on John Street; and brick and stone Georgian for the Rondout National Bank on the East Strand and Ferry Street (completed 1929; not extant). His other buildings in the city include the former Jewish Community Center (1925), Twaalfskill Golf Club House (1926), the Savings and Loan Association of Kingston (267 Wall Street, c. 1939; not extant), Uptown Post Office, and a twelve-room addition (1929) and vocational building (1937-1938) at Kingston High School.

A charter member of Kingston Rotary Club, Betz belonged to several other social organizations. He retired about 1960 and died December 22, 1962, at age eighty-one.

GEORGE E. LOWE (1890-1966)

George E. Lowe was born in Port Ewen on July 1, 1890, the son of Elmer and Margaret Bigler Lowe. His obituary in the *Freeman* (September 6, 1966) records that "he attended Ulster Academy and took a course in architectural drawing and design, receiving his diploma in 1912. He was employed for a time in the offices of the late Arthur C. Longyear, the late Myron S. Teller and the late Thomas P. Rice." Lowe's notable works in Kingston include the Governor Clinton Hotel, portions of Kingston Hospital, and the Home for the Aged. Along with Myron Teller and Gerard Betz, he was a member of the architectural commission responsible for the redesigning of city hall after the 1927 fire. He was also the local architect associated with theatre specialist Douglass Hall in the building of the Broadway Theatre, and he redesigned the interior of St. John's Episcopal Church when it was moved to Albany Avenue. Other designs by Lowe were executed in Catskill, Windham, and Cornwall.

Active in Trinity Methodist Church, Lowe was also a Mason, Shriner, and charter member of the Kingston Kiwanis Club. In 1914 he married Margaret F. Mambert. He died September 6, 1966, and is buried in Wiltwyck Cemetery.

ALBERT EDWARD MILLIKEN (C. 1900-1978)

"Ned" Milliken studied architecture at Cornell University (Class of 1924), where he also gained useful experience as a captain of field artillery in R.O.T.C. His early professional experience included a stint in New York as assistant to Norman Bel Geddes, the stage set designer. After the 1927 city hall fire, Milliken was employed by the architectural commission to do all drawings and superintend construction of the rebuilding. In 1931, as a designer in the Division of Architecture, State Department of Public Works, Milliken planned the Armory on North Manor Avenue. The near-absence of ornament was "not intended to be 'modern' or 'modernistic' design ... but is a frank attempt to use common brick in as simple and economic a manner as possible." (*Freeman*, January 31, 1931) In 1935 he opened his architectural office in Kingston, and three years later the Woodstock Playhouse was built according to his plans.

During World War II, Milliken served in the Army Corps of Engineers and Air Corps. His engineering projects included construction of the Army Air Base in Bermuda and plans for the Photo Reconnaissance Laboratories of the Eighth Air Force in England.

In 1945 he was released from active duty as a major, and resumed his architectural practice in Kingston.

Milliken's Kingston houses completed by 1950 include the dignified Tudor house of Joseph Levine (1939-1940) on Mountain View Avenue, and several Colonial Revival residences: a house with doctor's office for Emil S. Goodyear, M.D., at 61 Maiden Lane; the Thomas V. Coffey house at 330 Hurley Avenue; and the William T. Fuller house on Noone Lane.

His Fuller house represented a compromise between the Colonial Revival and modernism. The 1946 design for the Pilgrim Furniture Company office and factory on Greenkill Avenue more thoroughly embraced modernism. The façade of the one-story office section, facing South Prospect Street, is sleekly horizontal with its band of windows set into glass blocks and its metal-banded entrance canopy. Also after the war, Milliken designed a showroom for the streamlined Tucker automobile, but, unfortunately, Preston Thomas Tucker's experimental car was never produced in quantity. Milliken's career after 1950 was busy and productive until his death in 1978.

GLOSSARY

ANTA. A pier or thickened end of a wall that forms one side of a Greek classical porch.

BALUSTRADE. A rail and the row of posts that support it.

CORBEL. A bracket projecting from the face of a wall and generally used to support an arch or cornice.

CORINTHIAN. The most ornate of the three orders of Greek classical architecture. Its columns have capitals with carved acanthus leaves.

CRENELATED BATTLEMENT. A notched defensive parapet.

DISTYLE IN ANTIS. In Greek classical architecture, two columns placed between antae.

DORIC. The simplest of the three orders of Greek classical architecture. Its columns have capitals with a square slab.

DRIP MOLDING. A projecting molding that protects an opening below from rainwater.

ENTABLATURE. In classical architecture, the horizontal moldings resting on the capital and including the architrave, frieze, and cornice.

GABLE ROOF. A roof with one slope on each side of the central ridge.

GAMBREL ROOF. A roof with two slopes on each side of the central ridge.

HIPPED ROOF. A roof with a sloping surface on each of the four sides of the building.

IONIC. One of the three orders of Greek classical architecture. Its columns have capitals with spiral scroll shapes.

JERKINHEAD. A roof clipped off at the ends of the central ridge.

MODILLION. An ornamental bracket used in a series under a classical cornice.

ORIEL. A projecting bay window supported from below by brackets, usually on an upper story.

PALLADIAN WINDOW. A three-part window, the outer two parts rectangular, the central part having an arched top. Named for the Italian Renaissance architect Andrea Palladio.

PEDIMENT. A wide, low-pitched triangular gable surmounting the façade of a classical building.

PENT ROOF. A roof of a single slope projecting slightly from the wall between two stories.

PERGOLA. An arbor or passageway with a roof of trelliswork.

PILASTER. A flattened column attached to and projecting slightly from a wall.

QUATREFOIL. An ornament with four lobes.

QUOIN. An accented rectangular block at the corner of a building.

RUSTICATED. Rough-textured masonry, with deep joints between the rough-surfaced blocks.

SPANDREL. A panel between a window on one story and a window on a story directly above or below.

TREFOIL. An ornament with three lobes.

TRIGLYPH. A vertical three-pronged molding in a Doric frieze.

ACKNOWLEDGMENTS

This guidebook would not have been written without the constant and generous encouragement and assistance of Jane Kellar, Executive Director of the Friends of Historic Kingston. Patricia Murphy of the Friends has been a wonderful resource throughout, and especially in the early walking and driving survey of the city that she, Jane Kellar, and I took to create a preliminary list of buildings for the guidebook. Annon Adams, though a Poughkeepsie resident, spent countless hours reading microfilm of nineteenth-century Kingston newspapers and wrote comprehensive and useful notes. Some years ago, Frances Gale also gave me detailed notes from her reading of Kingston newspapers, as did a student, Kathleen Wood. Edwin M. Ford, City of Kingston Historian, has long taken a kindly interest in my study of regional architecture, and now he has answered any number of questions and solved several mysteries.

I have been fortunate to be able to speak with several men who worked for early-twentieth-century Kingston architects: Alfred P. Marquart for Charles Keefe; the late Charles G. Ellis for Myron Teller; and Thomas H. Clancy for Gerard Betz. Robert E. Milliken lent photos of early works by his father, Albert E. Milliken. The late T. Jay Rifenbary was a memorably enthusiastic guide to buildings erected by his father, Jay W. Rifenbary, for various architects. T. Jay Rifenbary introduced me to the late Harry Halverson, who spoke with me about his career. Harry Halverson's daughter, Nancy Halverson Schless, an architectural historian, entrusted me with a box of her father's papers after his death.

Others who have been generous in providing information and various kinds of assistance include: George Allen, Eli and Susan Basch, Raymond L. Caddy, Roselyn Daniell, Susan DeMaio, Joseph Diamond, George Hutton, Paul Kellar, Marilyn Gadd Koster, John Lenz, Donna Light, Suzanne Lown, Glendon Moffett, Robert Slater, Abigail Sturges, Dirck Teller, Lowell Thing, Dell Upton, and Wendell Tripp. The staffs of the Kingston Area Library, Sojourner Truth Library at SUNY New Paltz, New-York Historical Society, Avery Library at Columbia University, and Senate House State Historic Site have always been helpful. I would like to extend particular thanks to Carol Johnson and Marion Ryan at the Elting Memorial Library in New Paltz, Julie McKelvey and Phyllis Crawford at the Ulster County Historical Society, Allynne Lange at the Hudson River Maritime Museum, and Eric Roth at the Huguenot Historical Society in New Paltz. The splendid photos of Kingston today are the work of James Bleecker. Rick Umble of Ulster County Information Services prepared the maps. Ruth Elwell has contributed the index. The Preservation League of New York State has kindly permitted the publication here of my essay on Charles S. Keefe that appeared in a slightly different form in its September 1985 *Newsletter*. Deborah Allen and Steve Hoare of Black Dome Press have consistently offered sage counsel and have handled this complex project with extraordinary care, Carol Clement created a fitting and artistic design, and the efforts of proofreaders

Matina Billias, Rebecca Minew, and Ed Volmar were invaluable. I am grateful, too, for John Winthrop Aldrich's foreword with his impassioned plea for the preservation of Kingston's architectural heritage.

My wife, Sally M. Rhoads, has been my companion and advisor in countless expeditions from New Paltz to explore the architecture of Kingston. Kingstonians owe her thanks, as I do, for discovering more than twenty years ago hundreds of architectural drawings and several boxes of correspondence from Charles Keefe's office.

This book is made possible with public funds from the New York State Council on the Arts, a state agency, and I wish to thank particularly the guidance of Anne Van Ingen, Director of Architecture, Planning and Design. The Friends of Historic Kingston has most generously provided funds essential for this publication, and also gratefully acknowledged are the grants provided by the Jay E. Klock and Lucia de L. Klock Foundation of Kingston, and by the Rondout Savings Bank.

Many owners and occupants of buildings in Kingston have provided a welcome and information. I wish it were possible to list them by name.

ABOUT THE AUTHOR

WILLIAM B. RHOADS, Professor of Art History at the State University of New York at New Paltz, earned his Ph.D. in architectural history at Princeton University in 1975. He is the author of THE COLONIAL REVIVAL (1977), and contributed to CHARMED PLACES: HUDSON RIVER ARTISTS AND THEIR HOUSES, STUDIOS AND VISTAS (1988). Rhoads has lectured and written extensively about the architecture and art of the Hudson Valley and Catskill regions.

SELECTED BIBLIOGRAPHY

Much of the information in this guidebook derives from Kingston and Rondout directories published from 1857 to the present, and available at the Kingston Library. The same library has microfilm of Kingston and Rondout newspapers. Annon Adams provided extensive notes on those published between 1865 and 1886. With the help of annual summaries of local events published in the *Daily Freeman*, I have concentrated on the years 1904 to 1951.

Allen, George. "Of the Old School" [District School No. 8], *Midtown Sentinel*, vol. 1, no. 4, 2002, 1-5.

Art Work of Ulster County. Chicago: W. H. Parish Publishing Co., 1893.

Bacon, Edgar. *The Hudson River*. New York: G. P. Putnam's Sons, 1907.

Barricklo, Kenneth Hewes. *Historic Structure Report. The Matthewis Persen House.* Kingston: County of Ulster, 2000.

Beers, F. W. *County Atlas of Ulster*. New York: Walker and Jewett, 1875.

Benepe, Barry, ed. *Early Architecture of Ulster County*. Kingston: Junior League of Kingston, 1974.

Blumin, Stuart M. *The Urban Threshold*. Chicago: University of Chicago Press, 1976.

Clearwater, Alphonso T. *The History of Ulster County, New York*. Kingston: W. J. Van Deusen, 1907.

Commemorative Biographical Record of Ulster County, New York. Chicago: J. H. Beers, 1896.

De Lisser, Richard Lionel. *Picturesque Ulster: The City of Kingston*. Kingston: Styles and Bruyn, 1896.

DeWitt, William C. *People's History of Kingston*. New Haven: Tuttle, Morehouse and Taylor, 1943.

Fowler, Orson Squire. *The Octagon House*. New York: Dover, 1973. Originally published 1853 as, *A Home for All, or the Gravel Wall and Octagon Mode of Building*.

Hendricks, Howard. *The City of Kingston*. Kingston: Board of Trade, 1902.

Hickey, Andrew S. *The Story of Kingston*. New York: Stratford House, 1952.

Historic American Buildings Survey, National Park Service.

Hoes, Roswell Randall. *The Old Court Houses of Ulster County, New York*. Kingston: Freeman Publishing, 1918.

Huey, Paul R. "Archaeological Exploration of the Louw-Bogardus Site, Kingston, New York," *Bulletin and Journal of Archaeology for New York State*, no.82, Fall 1981.

Kingston, N.Y. Illustrated and Descriptive. Kingston, 1906.

Kowsky, Francis R. *Country, Park & City: The Architecture and Life of Calvert Vaux*.

New York: Oxford University Press, 1998.

McAlester, Virginia and Lee. *A Field Guide to American Houses*. New York: Knopf, 1984.

McEntee, Jervis. Manuscript Diary. New-York Historical Society (available on microfilm through the Archives of American Art).

Malo, Paul. "The Architecture of the Stockade District, Kingston, New York." Report to the Kingston Historic Landmarks Preservation Commission, 1969.

Moffett, Glendon L. *Uptown-Downtown. Horsecars-Trolley Cars. Urban Transportation in Kingston, New York, 1866-1930*. Fleischmanns: Purple Mountain Press, 1997.

Murray, Stuart. *Thomas Cornell and the Cornell Steamboat Company*. Fleischmanns: Purple Mountain Press, 2001.

Partlan, Martha B. and Dorothy A. DuMond, *The Reformed Protestant Dutch Church of Kingston, New York*. Kingston, 1984.

Reflections: A Jewish Bicentennial Edition. Kingston: Temple Emanuel, 1976.

Reynolds, Helen Wilkinson. *Dutch Houses in the Hudson Valley before 1776*. New York: Dover, 1965. Originally published 1929.

Schneider, Gail. "A Beginning Investigation into the Afro-American Cemeteries of Ulster County, New York," *Afro-Americans in New York Life and History*, vol. 10, January 1986, 61-69.

Schoonmaker, Marius. *The History of Kingston, New York*. New York: Burr Printing House, 1888.

Steuding, Bob. *Rondout: A Hudson River Port*. Fleischmanns: Purple Mountain Press, 1995.

Sylvester, Nathaniel Bartlett. *History of Ulster County, New York*. Philadelphia: Everts & Peck, 1880.

Upjohn, Everard M. *Richard Upjohn Architect and Churchman*. New York: Da Capo, 1968. Originally published 1939.

Vaux, Calvert. *Villas and Cottages*. New York: Harper and Brothers, 1869.

Woods, Ron. *Kingston's Magnificent City Parks*. Kingston, 1992.

Zimm, Louise Hasbrouck, et al. *Southeastern New York*. 3 vols. New York: Lewis Historical, 1946.

PHOTO SOURCES

Most of the photographs in this guide were taken by James Bleecker in 2001. Other photos derive from the following sources:

Avery Architectural and Fine Arts Library, Columbia University in the City of New York: page 60.

Fair Street Reformed Church: page 70.

Friends of Historic Kingston: pages 11, 13, 22, 27 (lower right), 73, 115, 120, 128, 135, 140 (lower), 157, 159 (upper), 160, 164 (upper), 166 (both), 168 (lower).

Haviland-Heidgerd Historical Collection, Elting Memorial Library, New Paltz: pages 173 (upper), 174 (lower).

Hudson River Maritime Museum: page 134 (lower).

New-York Historical Society: page 133.

The William O'Reilly Collection: pages 26, 28, 42 (upper), 69, 76, 82, 92 (upper), 99, 100, 104, 105, 107, 114, 123 (lower), 140 (upper), 143, 144, 145, 158, 169 (both), 171 (upper), 172 (upper), 173 (lower), 175 (both).

William B. Rhoads: pages 20, 40, 41 (lower), 43, 44 (upper), 46, 55 (upper), 59, 64, 65, 74 (upper), 85 (lower), 86, 88, 96, 97, 103, 106 (upper), 113 (lower), 123 (upper), 126 (upper), 127, 137, 139, 146, 149 (upper), 151, 154, 165, 167 (both), 168 (upper), 170 (upper), 171 (lower), 174 (upper), 176 (both), 177 (both), 178.

Robert Slater: pages 29, 47, 50.

Sojourner Truth Library, SUNY New Paltz: pages 45, 163, 170 (lower), 172 (lower).

Stone Ridge Library: page 51 (lower).

Ulster Performing Arts Center: page 95.

David Wheatcroft Antiques: page 164 (lower).

INDEX